Occasional Paper No 75

Adam Buck's Greek Vases

Ian Jenkins

British Museum
1989

BRITISH MUSEUM OCCASIONAL PAPERS

Publishers: British Museum, Great Russell Street
London WC1B 3DG

Executive Editor: G. B. Morris

Production Editor: G. Bayliss

Distributors: British Museum Publications Ltd
46 Bloomsbury Street, London WC1B 3QQ

Occasional Paper No.75, 1989:

Adam Buck's Greek Vases
Ian Jenkins

ISBN 0 86159 075 9

ISSN 0142 4815

Orders should be sent to British Museum Publications Ltd. Cheques and postal orders should be payable to 'British Museum Publications Ltd' and sent to 46 Bloomsbury Street, London WC1B 3QQ. Access, American Express, Barclaycard/Visa cards are accepted.

CONTENTS

Page

Abbreviations

The initials ADT and JCB signify information supplied by A. D. Trendall and J. Burns; DvB, information given by Dietrich von Bothmer.

Beazley's lists

ABV: J. D. Beazley, Attic Black-Figure Vase-Painters (Oxford 1956).

ARV: Attic Red-Figure Vase-Painters (Oxford 1942).

ARV^2: Attic Red-Figure Vase-Painters (Second edition, 1963).

Para: Paralipomena, Additions to Attic Black-Figure Vase-Painters (2nd ed. Oxford 1971).

Addenda: Beazley Addenda, Additional references to ABV, ARV^2 and Paralipomena, compiled by L. Burn and R. Glynn (Oxford 1982).

Trendall's Lists

LCS: A.D. Trendall, The Red-Figured Vases of Lucania, Campania and Sicily. 2 vols. (Oxford 1967).

RVAp: The Red-Figured Vases of Apulia. 2 vols. (Oxford 1978 and 1982).

RVP: The Red-Figured Vases of Paestum (British School at Rome 1987).

Other publications

AJA: American Journal of Archaeology.

BMMA: The Metropolitan Museum of Art Bulletin.

Bothmer: D. von Bothmer, 'The Death of Sarpedon', in The Greek Vase, edited by S.L. Hyatt (New York 1981) 63-80.

Brommer: F. Brommer, Vasenlisten zur griechischen Heldensage III (1973).

Cambitoglou: A. Cambitoglou, 'Some Campanian Vases in Manchester', Memoirs and Proceedings of the Manchester Literary and Philosophical Society, vol 90 (1948-49) 1-17.

Dörig: J. Dörig, Art Antique - Collections Privées de Suisse Romande (Geneva 1975).

Dubois-Maisonneuve: M. Dubois-Maisonneuve, Introduction à l'Étude des Vases Antiques (Paris 1817).

Edwards: E.J. Edwards, Two Ancient Greek Vases known as the Capo di Monte and Actaeon, now on view (by permission) in the British Museum (Chiswick Press n.d.).

Greifenhagen: A. Greifenhagen, 'Griechische Vasen auf Bildern des 19 Jahrhunderts', Sitzungsberichte der Heidelberger Akademie der Wissenschaften (Heidelberg 1978).

Haspels: C.H.E. Haspels, *Attic Black-Figured Lekythoi* (Paris 1936).

Jenkins: I.D. Jenkins, 'Adam Buck and the Vogue for Greek Vases', *The Burlington Magazine* 130 (June 1988) 448-457.

JHS: *The Journal of Hellenic Studies*.

Landes and Laurens. *Les vases à mémoire*: Les collections de céramique grecque dans le midi de la France (Lattes 1988).

Lugt: F. Lugt, *Repértoire des Catalogues de Ventes Publiques* 1600-1900. 3 vols. (La Haye 1938-1964).

Metzger: H. Metzger, *Recherches sur L'Imagerie Athénienne* (Paris 1965).

Michaelis: A. Michaelis, *Ancient Marbles in Great Britain* (Cambridge 1882).

Millin: A.L. Millin, *Monuments Antiques, Inédits ou Nouvellement Expliqués*. 2 vols. (Paris 1802-6).

Millingen: J. Millingen, *Ancient Unedited Monuments, Painted Greek Vases*. (London 1823).

Moses (1814): H. Moses, *A Collection of Antique Vases, Altars, Paterae, Tripods, Candelabra, Sarcophagi etc*. (London 1814).

Moses: H. Moses, *Vases from the Collection of Sir Henry Englefield Bart*. (London 1819).

Neugebauer: K.A. Neugebauer, *Führer durch das Antiquarium, Staatliche Museen zu Berlin vol. 2: Vasen* (Berlin 1932).

OM Leiden: *Oudheidkundige Mededelingen uit het Rijksmuseum van Oudheidente Leiden*.

Passeri: J.B. Passeri, *Picturae Etruscorum in Vasculis*. 3 vols. (Rome 1767-75).

Robertson: C.M. Robertson, *Greek, Etruscan and Roman Vases in the Lady Lever, Art Gallery, Port Sunlight* (Liverpool 1987).

Tillyard: E.M.W. Tillyard, *The Hope Vases* (Cambridge 1923).

van Hoorn: G. van Hoorn, *Choes and Anthesteria* (Leiden, 1951).

Vermeule: C.C. Vermeule, *Sir John Soane's Museum. Catalogue of the Classical Antiquities*. 2 vols. (London 1953, revised Boston 1975).

Waagen: G.F. Waagen, *Treasures of Art in Great Britain*. 4 vols. (London 1854-57).

Walpole: R. Walpole, *Travels in Various Countries of the East; being a continuation of Memoirs Relating to European and Asiatic Turkey*. 2 vols. (London 1818-1820).

ADAM BUCK'S GREEK VASES

The Irish-born watercolourist Adam Buck (1759-1833) is best known for his portrait miniatures and as a fashionable illustrator. Although the Regency vogue for Greek vases is self-evident in Buck's illustrative work and occasionally in his portraits, his serious interest in vases for their own sake has, until recently, been forgotten.[1] In 1811, however, Adam Buck issued a prospectus advertising his intention of publishing one hundred engravings from his drawings after Greek vases, then to be found in a number of English private collections. In this, the hey day of the Greek Revival, the passion for collecting Greek vases was running high. Buck hoped, therefore, to emulate the success of Sir William Hamilton's two major publications that had done so much to promote the taste for Greek, or, as they were commonly called, 'Etruscan' vases.[2] If he had succeeded then he would have been among the first to reproduce accurate, if idealised, representations of Greek vases. In fact the project failed, and Buck's original drawings are now preserved in a bound volume in the library of Trinity College, Dublin.[3]

Buck's Greek vases were to have been published in ten monthly instalments of ten engravings each. A copy of the prospectus survives in the Department of Greek and Roman Antiquities in the British Museum, together with the first instalment of plates. The prospectus is inscribed in Buck's hand with the name of Sir Joseph Banks and must have been sent to the distinguished President of the Royal Society by the artist. A further copy of the prospectus and two sets of the plates survive at Castle Howard, the prospectus being inscribed with the name of Frederick Howard, 5th Earl of Carlisle who was to have been the dedicatee of the work.[4] Buck's hope of publication was not realised, and after his death the original drawings and such of the engravings as had been executed passed into the library of A. J. Hope, son of the more famous Thomas Hope of Deepdene.[5] It was probably then that the drawings were mounted onto backing sheets and bound into a single volume including Buck's sketch for a printed title page. At the Hope sale of 1917 the volume was purchased by a bookseller and was acquired from him by the art historian Thomas Bodkin.[6] He did a certain amount to advertise his discovery and this brought the drawings to the attention of J. Beazley at a time when he was in the process of compiling his lists of Attic red-figure vase-painters.[7]

A letter from Beazley to Bodkin is inserted into the Dublin volume and is reproduced below. Beazley was allowed to borrow the drawings in the Summer of 1919, but no record of his response to them has so far been discovered among his papers in the Beazley Archive at Oxford, nor does he refer to the drawings in any of his published lists. Since, however, Beazley's primary interest at this date was in the attribution of vases to hands, he may have been frustrated in this by Buck's overt stylisation of the originals. Further, he will have been disappointed at the large proportion of South-Italian vases represented among the drawings. As A. Trendall readily acknowledges, Beazley was not at this time uninterested in South-Italian vase painting; it is only in more recent years, however, that owing to Trendall's own industry, 'Italiote' vases, as Beazley called them, have come into their own and have received the same rigorous analysis of style as he himself applied to the products of Attic workshops.[8]

After this brief airing, Buck's Greek vases were destined to be forgotten once more, and when the British Museum declined to buy them, Bodkin presented the volume to the library of Trinity College Dublin, where they have remained largely ignored. They are worthy of our attention, however, for two main reasons: firstly, because of the insight they afford into the history of taste and, in particular, the information they provide about British interest in vases during the Regency Greek Revival; and, secondly, because they provide the only record of a number of vases that may now be termed 'lost', as well as giving previously unknown find-spots and collector's provenances for a number of others. The drawings of these lost vases are reproduced here together with some for which published illustrations are not easily available. The catalogue lists the complete series of vases featured in the Dublin volume, and this is prefaced by notes on the collectors whose vases feature in the drawings. Broader aspects of the history of taste and collecting with reference to Buck's drawings are treated elsewhere.[9]

The volume itself comprises one hundred and sixty-two pen and ink outlines bound together with thirty-two engravings. Some of the drawings are enhanced with a wash of sepia, or maroon where it was necessary to indicate the use of added purple in black-figured vase-painting. In the finished engravings Buck consciously simplified the drawing into a crisp black and white outline; added colour in the drawing is represented in the engraving by aquatinting, and the artist usually added a signature, the date and the person to whom the original vase belonged. The illustrations reproduced here, for the sake of economy from microfilm, do not convey the quality of the original drawings; they are intended only as a record of the paintings shown in them.

Buck's original numbering is often visible on the drawings or engravings, but in compiling this catalogue the author has introduced an independent numbering sequence. This consists of a folio number which is followed by the number of the individual drawing or engraving; e.g. 1:1. Where both the drawing and the engraving exist of the same subject, then the second number is the same, but drawing and engraving are distinguished by use of a following letter (a) or (b); e.g. 1:1(a) for the drawing and 1:1(b) for the engraving. Sometimes two separate drawings have been mounted in the volume as one; e.g. folio 54. Here the second number is the same for both drawings but, since they show different subjects, they are distinguished by a following Roman numeral in lower case; thus: 54: 60(i) and (ii).

Notes

1. This is the second of two publications in which Buck's interest in Greek vases is discussed. For a full bibliography on the artist and his times, therefore, see I. D. Jenkins, 'Adam Buck and the Vogue for Greek Vases' in The Burlington Magazine 130 (June 1988) 448-457.

2. See entry for Hamilton in Notes on Collectors; see also M. Vickers, 'Value and Simplicity: Eighteenth Century Taste and the Study of Greek Vases' in Past and Present 116 (1987) 98-137.

3. Trinity College Dublin Ms. 2031.

4. Hitherto only the British Museum's copy has been known and it was this that had been consulted by Beazley, and of which he makes mention in his published lists of Attic red-figured vases: see the letter from Beazley to Thomas Bodkin, published here.

5. D. Watkin, Thomas Hope 1769-1831 and the Neo-Classical Idea (London 1968).

6. A. Denson, Thomas Bodkin (Printed privately in Dublin, 1966) 77.

7. These resulted in Attische Vasenmaler des rotfigurigen Stils (Tübingen 1925), superseded in 1942 by the first edition of Attic Red-Figure Vase-Painters.

8. A. D. Trendall, 'Beazley and South Italian Vase Painting' in D. Kurtz (ed.), Beazley and Oxford, Lectures delivered at Wolfson College, Oxford on 28 June 1985. Oxford University Committee for Archaeology Monograph no 10 (Oxford 1985) 31-42.

9. I. D. Jenkins, The Burlington Magazine op. cit. (note 1).

NOTES ON COLLECTORS

John Proctor Anderdon (also Anderson, 1760-1846) Cat. nos. 13:11-15:14.
Lived at Farley Hall, near Reading. Originally a partner in the mercantile firm of Anderdon and Manning. Visited Italy in 1827 where he acquired a number of fine paintings.

British Museum Department of Prints and Drawings, Collectanea Bibliographica, vol. 2, Alc-And. The scene of a black-figured lekythos in the collection of J. P. Anderdon is reproduced by Moses, (1814) pl. 1.

Thomas Bruce, 7th Earl of Elgin (1766-1841). Cat. nos. 55:61 i, ii and possibly iii, 56:62 iv, 57:63 i and ii, 58:64-63:70, 64:72, 77:93.

Appointed as British Ambassador to the Sublime Porte 1799. Acquired vases from Greece as a result of the operations of his agents in Athens and also from Sicily. A number of vases came to the British Museum with the acquisition of the Elgin collection of 1816. Others went to Broomhall (Elgin's Scottish home), where they remained until 1957 when the collection was sold and dispersed.

C. Vermeule, AJA 59 (1955) 132; Vermeule and D. von Bothmer, AJA 63 (1959) 141-142; W. St. Clair, Lord Elgin and the Marbles (Oxford 1983); Jenkins, 453-4.

Adam Buck. v. s. passim. Cat. nos. 48:52 - 52:58, 71:83 iii, 72:86 iii.
Lugt lists two sales of Buck's collection, both posthumous, and neither includes vases: 4-6 March 1834 (Southgate); 30 July 1851 (Sander Pratt).

Arthur Champernowne (d. 1819). Cat. no. 16:15.
M. P. for Saltash 1806. His artworks were sold by Christie's, 29-30 June 1820 together with residue from the earlier Coghill sale of 1819. Only Coghill vases feature in the catalogue, however, and the Champernowne bell-krater is not listed.
J. L. Vivian, The Visitations of the County of Devon (Exeter 1895) 164.

William Chinnery. Cat. no. 75:91 ii.
Brother of the landscape painter George Chinnery (1766-1846). The Chinnery vases were sold by Christie's, 3-4 June 1812.

Michaelis 163. See also Payne Knight, below.

William Danby (1752-1833). Cat. no. 115:143.
Miscellaneous writer ... rebuilt almost entirely his mansion of Swinton Park, Yorkshire from designs by James Wyatt and John Foss of Richmond: Dictionary of National Biography.

Edward Davies Davenport (1778-1847). Cat. nos. 29:31-30:32, 72:85, 73:87-88
Mrs Bromley Davenport of Capesthorne Hall, near Macclesfield describes him as the family rebel: 'He was a militant Whig in this staunch Tory family, and as Member of Parliament for Shaftesbury faced his father (Davies Davenport III) across the floor of the house from 1826-1830'.

Edward Davenport is said to have collected antiquities on the Grand Tour in Italy. A number of sculptures and vases are preserved at Capesthorne but the vases drawn by Buck are not among them. Some may have been destroyed when Capesthorne Hall was burned in the mid-nineteenth century.

Lady Bromley Davenport, Capesthorne (Derby second edition 1957); C. Vermeule and D. von Bothmer AJA 63 (April 1959) 146-9; D. von Bothmer, Ancient Vases (n.d.) - a handlist to the Capesthorne vases.

James Edwards (1757-1816). Cat. nos. 35:38-39:43.
Bibliographer and bookseller - Edwards and Sons, Pall Mall, London.

Nine vases were offered for sale, together with his valuable library, by R. H. Evans, 5 April, 1815. An annotated copy of the catalogue in the library of the Victoria and Albert Museum records that lots 6-9 were 'put up' at the following prices: £200, £300, £100 and £700 respectively. Lots 7 and 9 (Cat. nos. 35:39, 37:41-39:43) remained in the family until the end of the last century: E. J. Edwards, Two Ancient Greek Vases known as the Capo di Monte and Actaeon now on view (by permission) in the British Museum (Chiswick Press n.d.). Shortly after the vases were displayed in the British Museum at least the volute-krater (Lot 9) was exported to America. Before 1899 it was in the T. B. Clarke collection: American Art Gallery Sale Catalogue, February 15-18, 1899 no. 424. It is now in The Metropolitan Museum of Art, New York. The history and importance of this vase is discussed in detail in Jenkins, 455. The so-called Actaeon vase (Lot 7), a bell-krater, was drawn by Adam Buck and the reverse features in the Dublin volume. It too is now in The Metropolitan Museum of Art.

See also a letter preserved in the British Museum Central Archives, Original Papers, vol. 20, 23 March 1839, in which E. J. Edwards offers the volute-krater to the Museum for £600.0.0. He remarks that this sum is considerably below the amount of the original purchase by Mr Edwards and also below the sum offered at the time of the sale of his library when it was withdrawn, and that, ... the number of the vases which have been found lately, have contributed to lessen the value of these curiosities in a very great degree. (This last is a reference to the glut of vases that had found their way onto the market following the discovery of the vase-rich cemeteries of southern Etruria.) The letter also tells us that having been withdrawn from the 1815 sale, the vase was entrusted for safe-keeping to Lord Northwick (see John Rushout, below).

C. A. G. Goede, The Stranger in England vol. 3 (1807), 3-7; Dictionary of National Biography; and see also Michaelis, 163 who confuses the history of Edwards's volute-krater with the Cawdor Vase (Soane, below); Jenkins, 454-5.

Sir Henry Englefield (1752-1822). Cat. nos. 53:59-54:60 i and, possibly, ii; 56:62 i and ii.
The Dictionary of National Biography describes him as an antiquary and scientific writer. He acquired vases at the Cawdor (1800), Chinnery (1812) and Coghill (1819) sales. The collection was sold by Christie's, 6 March, 1823. A volume illustrating vases from his collection was produced by Henry Moses: Vases from the Collection of Sir Henry Englefield Bart. (London 1819).

Sandford Graham (1788-1852). Cat. nos. 56:62 iii, 65:73-69:81.
Member of Parliament. He collected vases during travels in Greece, sold by King and Lochée, 23 May 1815, which are described as having been found in Attica, '... and principally on the left-hand side of the Antient Paved Way leading from Athens to Thebes'.

Michaelis, 160; G. P. Judd, Members of Parliament 1734-1832 (Yale 1972) 210; Jenkins, 453.

Thomas Gwennap (d. circa 1845). Cat. nos. 32:34-34:37 i and ii, 71:83 ii; 72:84.
He was a Bond Street dealer who sold off his stock, Greenwood, 13-19 June 1806, having 'entered into a concern of a different nature'. The sale included a variety of items with some 'Etruscan vases'. The catalogue entries are not sufficiently descriptive, however, to positively identify any of the vases as those drawn by Buck. At the posthumous sale of his artworks, Foster, 17 April, 1845, no vases were included in the catalogue.

Sir William Hamilton (1730-1803). Cat. nos. 90:106 i, ii and iii; 91:107; 92:109 i and ii -94:111; 96:113-112:137.

He amassed two vase collections during thirty-seven years residence in Naples and Sicily as British Envoy Extraordinary to the Bourbon Court of Ferdinand IV. The first collection, illustrated in D'Hancarville's, Collection of Etruscan, Greek and Roman Antiquities from the Cabinet of the Hon. Wm. Hamilton (4 vols, Naples 1766 [68] - 76), was purchased for the British Museum in 1772. The second Hamilton collection was illustrated in Collection of Engravings from Ancient Vases mostly of Pure Greek Workmanship, discovered in Sepulchres in the Kingdom of the Two Sicilies (4 vols. and suppl. Naples 1791-5). The preparation of the line engravings in this publication was overseen by J. H. W. Tischbein. The second collection was embarked on board the Colossus for England in 1798 when Napoleon's invasion of Italy necessitated retreat from Italy. Part of the collection was lost at sea but the bulk reached England safely and was sold in 1801 to Thomas Hope. A large number of 'lost' fragments have since been retrieved from the wreck of the Colossus in underwater excavations supervised by A. Birchall. These are now in the British Museum.

B. Fothergill, Sir William Hamilton, Envoy Extraordinary, (London 1969); R. Morris, HMS Colossus (London 1979).

John Hinxman (d. 1848). Cat. nos. 45:49-46:50; 76:92.
Collector of paintings.

Frederick Howard, 5th Earl of Carlisle (1748-1825). Cat. nos. 18:18-28:29; 72:86 i and ii; 74:89.

Frederick Howard acquired his vases from Henry Tresham in 1811, in exchange for an agreement to endow Tresham with an annuity of £300 for life. Tresham had acquired his vases from two sources: he was resident in Rome from 1775 to 1789 and acquired a number of vases during this period; he is also said to have bought vases from a servant of Thomas Hope, thought to be the 'dross' of the second Hamilton collection purchased by Hope in 1801.

The 5th Earl died in 1825 and his vsaes were put up for sale at Christie's on 3 May 1826. A number of them remained unsold, however, and the best and most famous piece, the Paestan bell-krater, London F149, was withdrawn and remained at Castle Howard until it was acquired by the British Museum in 1890. Waagen described this vase in his Treasures of Art in Great Britain (vol. 3, 326), and also mentions sixteen others, which were placed on four high cabinets.

There are now no vases at Castle Howard. Duthie's manuscript inventory of 1881 lists twenty-one pieces: Castle Howard Archives H 2/2/3, Catalogue of Statuary, Marble Table Tops, Bronzes and Ivories.

Michaelis mentions only the Paestan bell-krater in his article for JHS vol 6 (1885) 33-41. (Michaelis's earlier account listing seventeen vases, in Ancient Marbles, 332 was taken from Waagen, since he had not himself visited Castle Howard at that time.) A residue of vases seems to have survived at Castle Howard until relatively recent times; seven were sold in 1944: Catalogue of Old English and Modern Household Furniture, Carpets, China and Glass removed from Castle Howard and Bransdale Lodge, Yorkshire, 3 July, 1944, Lots 192, 344 and 345. (Five vases acquired from the Hope Sale of 1917 were resold by Francis Howard Esq. at Sotheby's Sale 14 March, 1929, Lots 84-88).

Richard Payne Knight (1750-1824). Cat. nos. 84:100-88:105.
Bequeathed his important collection of antiquities and drawings to the British Museum including just over fifty vases. The text of the letter to Lord Aberdeen of 13 June 1812, is quoted by R. Liscombe, Art Bulletin 61 (1979) 606, as follows: '... We collectors who have been preying upon each other's spoils lately like cray fish in a pond, which immediately begin sucking the shell of a deceased brother. Chinnery's vases went chiefly to Hope, Sir H. Englefield, Rogers and myself and brought good prices. It might be three of the most important to make the tops of my cases uniform, also three of [the Rt. Hon. Edmund] Burke's busts ....'

See also M. Clarke and N. Penny, The Arrogant Connoisseur (Manchester 1982) 70, espec. notes 44-5.

Brownlow North, Bishop of Winchester (1741-1820). Cat. nos. 17:16-17.
Said to have passed many years with his wife in Italy. His vases were most probably drawn at Winchester Palace, Chelsea.

Walsh Porter. Cat. no. 32:34.
His pictures were sold by Christie's, 22 March, 1803, when he was said to be going abroad. No vases are listed in the sale.

Samuel Rogers (1763-1855). Cat. nos. 1:1-12:10; 29:30; 114:140-141.
Banker and poet. In 1803 he laid out his new house at St. James's Place overlooking Green Park, in the style of Thomas Hope's Regency Greek revival. One of its features became the large collection of Greek vases, many of superb quality. These were sold upon his death by Christie's, together with the rest of his antiquities, books, paintings and furniture, 28 April, 1856 and eighteen following days. A list of purchaser's names and prices was printed subsequently.

P. Clayden, The Early Life of Samuel Rogers (1887) 448-9; Dictionary of National Biography. Michaelis, 154. Waagen, vol. 2, 73-4.

John Rushout, 2nd Lord Northwick (1770-1859). Visited Rome for eight successive years from 1792. Amassed a vast collection of important paintings, ancient sealstones and sundry antiquities including a few vases many of which were displayed at Thirlestane House, Cheltenham. The entire contents of the house were sold by Phillips, 26 July, 1859. A printed list of purchasers and prices was drawn up after the sale.

E. Brydges, Collins's Peerage of England vol. 8 (1812) 575. H. A. Doubleday and H. de Walden, The Complete Peerage, vol. 9 (1936) 752.

George Saunders (1762-1839). Cat. no. 43:47.
Architect. Designed the Townley Gallery at the British Museum. His proposed bequest of a cast of the Apollo Belvedere which was said to stand in his 'Museum' was refused by the British Musuem - Archives, Original Papers 33, 7 Aug. 1840. Dictionary of National Biography s.v.

Sir John Soane (1753-1837). Cat. nos. 40:44-42:44.
Architect and antiquary, Soane built up an undistinguished collection of vases from various sales, notably that of James Clark, Christie's, 9 June, 1802, at which he bought forty vases. Michaelis, 163, confuses Soane's acquisition of a South Italian volute-krater, at the Cawdor sale of 9 May 1800, with Edwards's 1000-guinea vase (see above). Vermeule, 561, draws our attention to an entry in Soane's Journal (no. 1) dated 9 May 1800: Paid Mr Taylor for vases bought at Lord Cawdor's sale with an individual item -£68.5.0. This is confirmed as the price paid for the Cawdor Vase by an entry against it as lot 64 in a copy of the Cawdor sale catalogue preserved in the Print Room of the British Museum. Neither Vermeule, however, nor Trendall, RVAp 906-7, fully succeed in dispelling the confusion initiated by Michaelis. The two vases have quite separate histories: the Cawdor Vase, as the sale catalogue emphatically states, came from the Vatican Library and will have been acquired by John Campbell from Rome - Jenkins, 454. This is corroborated by J. B. Passeri, vol.3,pls. 282-9. The Edwards vase was never in the papal collection but remained in southern Italy until it was brought to England.

Charles Townley (1737-1805). Cat. nos. 78:94-84:99; 91:108; 95:112i and ii, 113:138-9; 114:142.

Townley is best known for his collection of sculptures acquired upon his death by the British Museum. The remainder of the collection remained in the possession of Charles Townley's heirs until it was purchased by the Museum in 1814.

A Museum inventory (Officers Reports, The Principal Librarian, vol. 3, July 9, 1814) records the acquisition of sixty-one Greek vases 'of fine work' and 'two hundred of an inferior order'. Only some one hundred and sixty vases, or parts of vases, however, are featured in the departmental Register of Acquisitions.

G. Vaughan informs me that Townley purchased more than 100 'Etruscan vases' in Italy in 1772 and made a further acquisition of 29 from James Byres.

Sir Richard Westmacott (1775-1856). Cat. nos. 44:48, 70:82.
Sculptor.
Dictionary of National Biography s.v.

Christ Church
Oxford

April 23 1919

Letter from Beazley to Bodkin

Dear Sir

A friend has shown me a cutting from the Times Literary Supplement with a letter from you about the 'Greek Vases' of Adam Buck. As I have not been able to turn up the files of the Times, and as the cutting lacks the date, I do not know whether what I am going to write will be news to you or not, but I am writing all the same, in case you have not received the information from another quarter.

You wrote that you thought it likely that Buck issued a prospectus of his proposed publication and that it had not met with sufficient encouragement. A copy of this prospectus exists in the archaeological library of the Greek and Roman Department at the British Museum. The fly leaf reads: 'Proposals / for publishing by subscription / one hundred engravings / from paintings on / Greek vases, / which have never been published, / drawn and etched by Adam Buck, / from private collections now in England. // Dedicated to /the Earl of Carlisle.

There follows a quantity of matter in smaller print setting forth the qualifications of the artist, and the conditions of subscription. The date is June 1, 1811.

The plates are as follows: the descriptions are mine: I take from Buck the notice of the collections in which the vases were when he drew them.

1. 'In the collection of Thomas Hope, Esq.' This is from a Nolan amphora of about 480 BC which was until lately in the Deepdene collection. At the Deepdene sale in 1917 it was bought for the Museum of Providence, Rhode Island. Obverse, two warriors fighting; reverse, a third warrior. Love - name Kallias. (See now ARV^2 653,1.)

2. 'In the collection of John Hinxman, Esq.' The subject is a symposion. The vase seems to be Attic of the early fourth century.

3. 'In the collection of Samuel Rogers, Esq.' Evidently from a Nolan amphora. Obverse, a woman with phiale and oinochoe; reverse, a woman. Love - name Kleinias. I mentioned this vase, known to me from Buck's drawings only, in the Journal of Hellenic Studies, 34 (1914), p.224. no 7e, and attributed it to an anonymous artist whom I called the Meletos Painter, about 460 BC. See also my Attic Red-Figured Vases in American Museums, p.222 under Buck.

4. 'In the collection of the Earl of Carlisle - late of Henry Tresham, Esq, RA'. A woman with a (mirror?), and a [?] leaning on a pillar. Evidently from an Italiote vase of the fourth century.

5. In the same collection as the last. Eros seated on a rock, and a woman holding aphiale. This is perhaps the reverse of number 4.

6. 'In the collection of Samuel Rogers, Esq.' Nike driving a quadriga, preceded by a youth (Hermes?). Attic, early fourth century.

7. 'In the collection of Charles Townley, Esq.' Obverse, two women with castanets; reverse, another. This is from a small pelike now in the British Museum.

(E357), which I mentioned in JHS 32 (1912), p. 359, no. 22, and assigned to 'the Pan Painter'. About 480-475 BC.

8. 'In the collection of John Proctor Anderson esq.' Three women, Italiote.

9. 'In the collection of Thomas Hope, Esq.' Hermes pursuing a woman. From a lekythos of about 480-475 BC, which was lately in the Deepdene collection. (See now ARV^2 649, 44).

10. Two black-figured vases. The first in the collection of Edward Davenport, Esq.': fragmentary; quadriga; Theseus and the Minotaur. The second 'in the collection of Thomas Hope, Esq.': Herakles and Geryon, no doubt from a lekythos.

Each plate is inscribed: 'Drawn and etched and published March 31, 1812, by Adam Buck'.

These 'Proposals' are mentioned by Mr Salomon Reinach in the bibliography appended to volume 2 of his Repertoire des vases peints grecs et etrusques. The only copy known to him was that in the library of the Greek and Roman Department.

It is likely that your book of drawings contains the only record of a number of vases which have disappeared, like the Kleinias vase. It is true that Buck's plates give a very inaccurate idea of the style of the originals, though some of them are distinctly better than others. Very few drawings of his time are more than caricatures of the vase paintings which they profess to reproduce. But even so they are of considerable value for the archaeologist in cases where the originals are no longer accessible. It may also be said that for the archaeologist the drawing would be more use than the etching.

I do not know whether you would ever feel inclined to lend your book to the Bodleian Library or the Ashmolean Museum, where I could go through it and make notes on the vases which are otherwise unknown; but if you would, should appreciate your kindness very highly. If not, perhaps you will allow me to see the work if ever I come to Dublin?

Yours very truly

J. D. Beazley

Concordance:

Beazley Letter	Dublin Volume
2	45.49 (b)
3	1.1 (b)
4	24.26 (b)
5	23.25 (b)
6	6.5 (b)
7	80.95 (b)
8	14.12 (b)
10	72.85

CATALOGUE OF THE DRAWINGS

Title page: 'A/Collection/of Drawings/and/Engravings/ from/Paintings/ on Greek Vases/ drawn and etched/ by/ Adam Buck. /Selected/from Various Collections in England,/ London Printed by - / for Adam Buck' The date, 1832, is also given having been altered from the original, which is now illegible.

Folio 1:1(a) Drawing. 'Inscribed On the opposite sides of a Greek Vase, in the possession of Samuel Rogers. Watermark: J .Whatman 1809. 21 x 29 cm.

1(b) Engraving of same. Beazley letter no.3. Inscribed: 'Vol I. Mr/Rogers, 1'. Printed inscription in the bottom right corner is erased. 21 x 30 cm.

Attic R. F. amphora. ARV[2] 988, 13. Achilles Painter (formerly Meletos Painter). Rogers Sale, 489. Height given there 14 in. Thence Redfern.

2:2 (a) Drawing. Three women around a stele. 'A Greek vase in the possession of Samuel Rogers Esq. From the Gori Collection'. 27.5 x 33. 5 cm.

3:2 (b) Engraving of same. Inscribed: 'Drawn, Etched and Published by Adam Buck, March 31, 1812. A Greek vase in the collection of Samuel Rogers Esq'. 26 x 29.5 cm.

Campanian neck-amphora: LCS 458, 50, CA Workshop Rogers Sale 460. Thence Daniel Sharpe. Later A. J. Matheson esq., Tiverton in Devon. Sold Sotheby's 24 July 1967, no 229. Passeri, vol II, pl. 110, (ex Gori).

4:3. Drawing. Athlete (left) holding a strigil, woman (right) with fillet; between them a large kalathos on a chest. Inscribed: 'Mr Rogers'. 24 x 35 cm.

South-Italian R.F. ADT: 'Should be from a hydria, such scenes are popular in middle Apulian. Perhaps near the Iliupersis Painter'.

4:4. Drawing. Three women, one seated. Inscribed: 'Mr Rogers'. 25 x 34 cm.

Campanian oinochoe. LCS 490, 374, CA Workshop - Close to Painter of Copenhagen 244; once Hope: Tillyard 291, pl. 38.4.

5.5 (a) Drawing. Inscribed: 'Mr Rogers'. 19 x 28. 5 cm.

6:5 (b) Engraving of same. Beazley letter no. 6. Inscribed in pencil: 'Mr Rogers' and printed below: 'Drawn and Etched and Published, March 31, 1812 by Adam Buck. A vase in the collection of Samuel Rogers Esq.' 22. 5 x 38.5 cm.

Late Attic R. F. Probably Rogers Sale 467. Height given there 14 in. Thence Wilsher.

7:6. Drawing. Symposiasts, two youths reclining and a flute-girl standing. Inscribed: 'Mr Rogers.' 24.5 x 35.8 cm.

Late Attic R. F.

7:7. Drawing. Symposiasts, as above. Inscribed. 'Mr Rogers.' 21.7 x 33 cm. Late Attic R. F.

8:8 (a) Drawing. Four mounted warriors with hunting dogs. Inscribed: 'Mr Rogers.' 21.5 x 35 cm.

8:8 (b) Engraving of same. Inscribed: 'Drawn, etched etc. A Greek vase in the collection of William Chinnery Esq.' (Sic.). 18.5 x 35.5 cm.

Attic B. F. lekythos. Rogers Sale 490. Thence Daniel Sharpe. Later, Henry Sharpe. Sold at Sotheby's 24 February 1964: no. 98 with plate.

9.9 (a) Drawing. Marriage of Dionysos. Inscribed: 'A Greek vase in the possession of Samuel Rogers Esq. - with the following'. The shape, a bell-krater, is sketched in pencil above. 27.5 x 44.7 cm.

10:9 (b) Engraving of same. Inscribed: 'Drawn, etched etc. A Greek vase in the collection of Samuel Rogers Esq.' 21.2 x 52.5 cm.

11:10 (a) Drawing. Reverse of above. 'A Greek vase in the possession of Samuel Rogers Esq., with the foregoing'. A bell-krater with lugs is sketched above. 27.5 x 42.5 cm.

12:10 (b) Engraving of same. 'Drawn, etched etc. A Greek vase in the collection of Samuel Rogers Esq.' 20.5 x 52 cm.

Attic R. F. Compared by H.R.W. Smith with London E257 (ARV^2 604.50). Rogers Sale 399. Thence W. H. Forman Esq. Sold 1899 no. 356; later H. de Morgan, sale 1901, no. 401. Later Charles W. Gould; sold Am. Ant. Ass. 29 Oct. 1932, 575.

13:11. Drawing. Satyr (left) approaching woman crouching at a laver. 'John Proctor Anderson'. 24.5 x 34. 5 cm. Watermark on mounting sheet: J. Whatman 1840.

South-Italian R.F. ADT: 'I have some doubts about this one - the drapery hanging from the tree above is most unusual, but it has probably been stylised. It need not be South Italian'.

14:12 (a) Drawing. 'John Proctor Anderson'. 23.5 x 36 cm. Watermark on mounting sheet as 13:11 above.

14:12 (b) Engraving of same. Beazley letter no.8. Inscribed only with Buck's initials enclosed within a circle. 19.7 x 36.5 cm.

South-Italian R. F. ADT: 'Campanian, later CA or even possibly Boston Ready Painter'.

15:13. Drawing. Woman looking right with one foot resting on the side of an amphora. 'J. P. Anderson. Patera'. 18.5 x 18.2 cm. Watermark on mounting sheet: J. Whatman 1840.

South-Italian R. F. ADT: 'A similar subject appears on a Paestan cup in Leiden (OM Leiden 41 [1960] 48. pl. 1.) by the Boston Orestes Painter. The one in your illustration is by no means the same, nor would I think it to be Paestan from the drawing, but the subject is very alike'.

15:14. Drawing. Woman seated on a panther striding to the left. 'J. P. Anderson. This figure more delicate'. 21 x 21 cm.

South-Italian R. F.

16:15. Drawing. Herakles carrying Ploutos. 'Arthur Champernowne from Vatican Library -bell'. 22.7 x 34. 7 cm. Watermark on mounting sheet: J. Whatman 1840.

Berlin 31094. Attic R. F. bell-krater. ARV^2 1446, 2. The Pourtales Painter. Neugebauer 131, pl. 69. Spink and Sons, Greek and Roman Antiquities from Famous Private Collections (sample stock catalogue) July 1924.

17:16. Drawing. Two symposiasts, and recumbent Silenos beneath the couch. 'Bishop of Winchester'. 22.5 x 26 cm. Watermark on mounting sheet J. Whatman 1840.

South-Italian R.F.

17:17. Drawing. Three symposiasts and naked hetaira. 'Bishop of Winchester. Bell.' 20 x 35.5 cm.

South-Italian R.F. bell-krater.

18.18. Drawing. Sacrifice of a goat at a herm. 'Bell. Earl of Carlisle. Late Henry Tresham Esq. This and the following one plate'. 23.3 x 32.5 cm. Watermark on mounting sheet J. Whatman 1840.

Port Sunlight 5008. Campanian bell-krater. LCS Suppl. 3, 131 no 286b; Roberston, 44 no. 50, pls. 56-7. Carlisle Sale, 28. Later, Duke of Sutherland, Stafford House. Knight, Frank and Rutley Sale, 14, 15 and 25 July 1913, lot 398.1. Thence Lever.

ADT now informs me that I. McPhee thinks this vase to be Attic, and he would himself agree with this view.

18:19. Drawing. Eros at a herm with satyr seated (left), youth seated and woman standing (right). 21.8 x 34.7 cm.

Port Sunlight 5007. Late Attic bell-krater. ARV^2 1448, 4. The Toya Painter. Robertson 39 no. 41, pl.40. Carlisle Sale, 27. Later, Duke of Sutherland, Stafford House. Knight, Frank and Rutley Sale 14, 15 and 25 July, 1913, lot 416.2. Thence Lever.

19:20. Drawing. Two warriors with plumed helmets, one mounted, the other having just leapt down. 'Earl of Carlisle. Late Henry Tresham. Bell'. 23.5 x 32.8 cm. Watermark on mounting sheet: J. Whatman 1840.

South-Italian R. F. bell-krater. ADT: 'Should be Campanian?' Carlisle Sale, 26. Height given there 15 in.

19:21. Drawing. Woman (left) holding a Xylophone and youth seated right. 'Earl of Carlisle. Late Henry Tresham'. 23.5 x 27.5 cm.

South-Italian R. F. ADT: 'Certainly Apulian, bell-krater or pelike, Darian period'.

20:22. Drawing. Alcmene on the pyre. 'Bell. A Greek vase in the possession of the Earl of Carlisle - Late of Henry Tresham Esq. RA. The letters scratched not painted'. 28 x 42 cm. Watermark on drawing: Edmeads and Pine 1809; on mounting sheet: J. Whatman 1840.

London F149. Paestan bell-krater signed by Python. RVP 139, 239. pl. 88 Carlisle Sale, 36 (withdrawn). Purchased by the British Museum in 1890: JHS xi (1890) 225-230, pl.6.

21:23 (a). Drawing. Woman with flying drapery (left) pouring wine into a large phiale held by Oscan warrior seated right. 'Earl of Carlisle. Late Henry Tresham'. 20.3 x 28.3 cm.

21:23 (b). Engraving of same. Inscription erased. 19.5 x 30 cm.

South-Italian R. F. ADT: 'Certainly Apulian'. Carlisle Sale, 37 (Height given there 17½ in.).

22:24 (a). Drawing. Woman (left) seated on rock and turning back to look at woman standing right. 'Greek Praefericulum. Earl of Carlisle. Late Henry Tresham'. 20.2 cm x 27.2 cm. Watermark on mount: J. Whatman 1840.

22:24 (b). Engraving of same. Inscription erased. 20.2 x 27.5 cm.

Manchester IVE 29. Campanian oinochoe. LCS 527, 702, The Painter of Copenhagen 244; Cambitoglou, p.10 and 16, pl. 7. Carlisle Sale, 40.

23:25 (a). Drawing. 'Earl of Carlisle. Late Henry Tresham'. 19 x 26 cm. Watermark on mounting sheet: J. Whatman 1840.

23:25 (b). Engraving of same. Beazley letter no.5. Inscription erased. 19.8 x 26.2 cm.

South-Italian R. F. ADT: 'More likely to be Apulian than early Lucanian'. Carlisle Sale, 22.

24:26 (a). Drawing. 'Earl of Carlisle. Late Henry Tresham'. 19.7 x 24.8 cm. Watermark on mounting sheet: J. Whatman 1840.

24:26 (b). Engraving of same. Beazley letter no. 4. Inscription erased. 19.6 x 24.7 cm.

Reverse of 23:25.

25:27 (a). Drawing. Two female bathers and a youth. 'Greek Praefericulum. Earl of Carlisle. Late Henry Tresham. Engraved'. 19.8 x 29 cm.

25:27 (b). Engraving of same. No inscription. 19.8 x 30.2 cm.

South-Italian R. F. ADT: 'Very remarkable!'

26:28 (a) (i) Drawing. Warrior wearing a pilos seated on a rock (left), mounted with (ii) a woman enclosed within a circle. (Obverse and reverse of same vase?). 'Greek Praefericulum. Earl of Carlisle. Late H. Tresham. Engraved'. 19.5 x 42. cm (for the two, together).

27:28 (b). Engraving of same. The figures are transposed. No inscription. 20.5 x 35. 7 cm.

South-Italian R. F. ADT: 'Should be fairly early Campanian, probably from the workshop of the Cassandra Painter'. Carlisle Sale, 42?

28:29. Engraving. Youthful Dionysos seated right, woman standing left bending over him. Inscribed in pencil: 'Earl of Carlisle. Late Henry Tresham'. 20.2 x 24 cm.

South-Italian R. F. ADT: 'Should be mid-Apulian, probably a bell-krater'.

29:30. Drawing. Three warriors, one arming assisted by a woman. 'Mr Rogers'. 14.5 x 38.3 cm.

Attic B.F. lekythos. DvB: 'Should be Phanyllis Group B, Arming Lekythoi'. Rogers Sale, 387; height. 33.0 cm. Thence Miss Rogers.

29:31. Drawing. Herakles and Pholos. 'Mr Davenport. Reduce to same size'. 12.7 x 19.7 cm.

Attic B.F. Does not appear to be listed in Brommer, Vasenlisten 3. 178-9.

30:32. Drawing. Gigantomachy. 'Painting from Greek vase found in Sicily - Edward Davenport Esq.' 24.3 x 42.5 cm.

Attic B.F. DvB: Lekythos (Leagran).

31:33 (a). Drawing. Woman seated left, standing Eros right. 'Sir Waltham Wynne'. 18.5 x 26.5 cm.

31:33 (b). Engraving of same. Inscribed with Buck's initials enclosed in a circle. 20 x 25.5 cm

South-Italian R.F. ADT: 'Should be early Lucanian - probably by the Dolon Painter, to judge from the treatment of the woman's breasts and drapery'.

32:34. Drawing. Three warriors and a captive woman. 'A Greek vase in the possession of Mr Gwennap. Late Walsh Porter Esq. (bell)'. 25 x 40.5 cm.

South-Italian R.F. ADT: 'Apulian. This should be from a column - krater, but the woman prisoner is unusual; it is generally a man. For style cf. Prisoner Painter and related vases'.

33:35. Drawing. Woman standing in naiskos and three women around. 'A Greek vase in the possession of Mr Gwennap'. 28.3 x 34.8 cm.

Possibly obverse of the following. The scene is illustrated in Dubois-Maisonneuve pl. 86, but the present whereabouts of the vase is not known.

33:36. Drawing. Funerary stele with woman left, youth right. 'Mr Gwennap'. 21.7 x 31.2 cm.

South-Italian R. F. ADT: 'Apulian. This looks to be reasonably early in the long series of such vases'.

34:37 (i). Drawing. Eros standing left with woman seated right, mounted with (ii) woman standing left and Eros seated right. Each is inscribed: 'A Greek Patera in the possession of Mr Gwennap. In one plate'.

Probably two sides of the same vase. South-Italian R.F.

35:38. Drawing. Satyr, Dionysos and two maenads bearing torches. 'James Edwards'. 22.7 x 33.4 cm.

Attic R. F. Edwards Sale, 6. Height. 50.8 x 45.7 cm. DvB: 'Should be a bell-krater or a calyx-krater'.

35:39. Drawing. Three draped youths. 'James Edwards. Reverse of the Actaeon'. 21.2 x 31.3 cm. Attic R.F. bell-krater. Reverse of New York 66.79. ARV^2 1154, 36; Para. 457,36. The Dinos Painter. Edwards, pl. 3 (a). Edwards sale, 7 (withdrawn; later Bastis Bronxville).

36:40. Drawing. Mounted Amazon (left) attacked by two Greek warriors. 'James Edwards. Bell'. 21.6 x 36.8 cm.

Attic R.F. bell-krater. ARV^2 1049, 1. Addenda 157. Christie Painter. Edwards Sale, 8; Later Maj. Sir R. Rasch, Bt. Sold Christie's 31 May, 1979 no. 323, pl. 69.

37:41. Drawing. Nike driving a quadriga to the left, led by Hecate with torches. 'Neck of Greek Vase. James Edwards'. 21.7 x 41 cm.

Neck of New York 56.171.63. (28/1) Apulian volute-krater. RVAp 907, 1. pl. 345. The Capodimonte Painter. Edwards Sale, 9. Later, T. B. Clarke (1890); then,William Randolph Hearst. Thence The Metropolitan Museum of Art, New York; Bothmer, BMMA March 1957 165ff.

38:42. Drawing. Above, assembly of gods; below, Greeks fighting Amazons. 'A Greek Vase in the collection of Jame Edwards. Formerly in the Royal Museum at Naples'. 32 x 45 cm.

Main scene of 37:41.

39:43. Drawing. Youth seated in naiskos, four figures grouped around. 'A Greek vase in the Collection of James Edwards Esq'. 29.2 x 44.5 cm. Watermark on drawing: J. Whatman 1811; on mounting sheet, J. Whatman 1840.

40:44. Drawing. Youth abducting woman, two nikai with quadriga. 'Neck of vase. Mr Soane'. 24.7 x 44.5 cm. Watermark on mounting sheet: J. Whatman 1840.

Neck of London, Soane Museum 101L, the so-called Cawdor Vase. Apulian R.F. volute-krater. RVAp 931, 119. Vermeule, 561-2, no. 538.

41:45. Drawing. Left, squatting Eros, right squatting Eros. 'This and the following one plate'. 16 x 32 cm. Watermark on mounting sheet: J. Whatman 1840.

Blinkers of Soane Museum 101L, 40.44 above.

42:46. Drawing. Oinomaos sacrificing to Zeus before the chariot-race. 'Mr Soane'. 31.2 x 39 cm. Watermark on mounting sheet: J. Whatman 1840.

Main scene of 40:44.

43:47. Drawing. Herakles in a chariot driven by winged Nike. 'A Greek vase in the collection of George Saunders Esq. Bell'. 26 x 42 cm. Watermark on mounting sheet: J. Whatman 1840.

Attic R.F. calyx-krater. ARV^2 1437, 13. The Upsala Painter. Property of Professor Sir Roger Mynors.

44:48. Drawing. Warrior seated with woman standing right, and Nike hovering left. 'R. Westmacott RA'. 24 x 31cm. Watermark on mounting sheet: J. Whatman 1840.

South-Italian R.F. ADT: 'Campanian, should belong to the post CA Painter area'.

45:49 (a). Drawing. 'John Hinxman'. 19 x 28. 3 cm.
45:49 (b). Engraving of same. Beazley letter no.2 'Drawn, etched and published March 31, by Adam Buck. A Greek vase in the possession of John Hinxman Esq.'

Late Attic R.F. bell-krater.

46:50. Drawing. Youthful Dionysos seated left with woman and youth standing right. 'John Hinxman'. 24.5 x 34 cm. Watermark on mounting sheet: J. Whatman 1840.

South-Italian R. F. ADT: 'Apulian?'.

47:51 (a). Drawing. Three women, one seated. 'Edmond Treherne'. 20 x 27.5 cm. Watermark on mount: J. Whatman 1840.
47:51 (b). Engraving of same. 20.2 x 2 cm.

South-Italian R. F. ADT: 'Probably Apulian, but the drawing is very stylised; the single stripe down the drapery is fairly common in early Apulian'.

48:52 (a). Drawing. Youth seated, with two women standing. 'Adam Buck. Bell'. 20 x 25 cm.
48:52 (b). Engraving of same. The artist's name on the drawing replaces an earlier inscription, while on the engraving there has been erased a now hardly readable inscription: 'Drawn, etched and published by Adam Buck, March 31, 1812. A Greek vase in the collection of the late Lord Henry Stuart'.
ADT: 'Probably Attic'.

49:53 (a). Drawing. Youthful Dionysos seated with maenad left, and satyr right. 'Adam Buck. Bell'. 21.5 x 26.6 cm.
49:53 (b). Engraving of same. 22 x 28 cm. Watermark on mounting sheet: J. Whatman 1840.

Cambridge, Fitzwilliam Museum GR.29.1952. Campanian R. F. bell-krater. LCS 410, 334. pl.163.3. Once Beldam collection. Transferred to the Fitzwilliam Museum from the Museum of Archaeology and Ethnology in Cambridge.

50:54 (a). Drawing. Left woman with jug and bowl, right Hermes. 'Adam Buck. Opposite sides'. 22.5 x 33.5 cm.
50:54 (b). Engraving of same. Inscribed with Buck's initials enclosed within circle. 20.2 x 30.3 cm.

Attic R. F. Nolan amphora. Possibly two sides of the same vase.

51:55. Drawing. Woman seated left, youth standing right. Eros hovers overhead. 'Adam Buck'. 20 x 27 cm.

South-Italian R. F. ADT: 'Apulian. This sort of scene is very common in pelikai of the Darius period - cf. RVAp pl. 189 etc. The Doric column on which the woman sits is also of frequent occurrence. Cf. RVAp 18. 166-167 etc'.

51:56. Drawing. Youthful Dionysos reclining, with satyr and two maenads. 'Adam Buck'. 22 x 32.7 cm. Watermark on mounting sheet: J. Whatman 1840.

South-Italian R. F. ADT: 'Presumably Apulian; cf. with the mask vases by the painter of Athens 1714, RVAp I, pl. 67'. For masks in Apulian vases see A.D. Trendall, forthcoming article in Studies Webster vol. 2.

52:57. Drawing. Woman leaning on a stele, and youthful Dionysos standing right. 'Adam Buck. Bell'. 23 x 38 cm.

South-Italian R. F. ADT: 'Apulian'.

52:58. Drawing. Three symposiasts reclining. 'Adam Buck. Bell'. 23 x 38 cm.

Late Attic? R. F. DvB: 'Possibly column-krater'.

53:59. Drawing. Woman seated left and youth standing right, at a stele. 'Facsimile of a Greek Vase in the Collection of Sir Henry Englefield. Found at Athens. Lac'. 20 x 29.5 cm.

Attic W.-G. lekythos. ARV[2] 1378, 36. The Reed Painter. Englefield Sale, 42: (Height given there 13in): '...brought from Athens by Sir William Gell'. Later Allason (Beazley). Moses, pl.39.

54:60. Two separate drawings of two different vases mounted side-by-side. The inscription runs over both drawings: 'Sir H. Englefield. Lac'. (i) Girl seated left, youth standing right 19.5 x 19.2 cm.

Campanian squat lekythos: LCS 302, 538. The Laghetto Painter. Englefield Sale, 38.1. (Height given there 8in). Thence Norton. Greifenhagen, 17 pls. 8-9. Moses, pl.33

(ii) Nike in flight holding a helmet. 19.5 x 22.7 cm.

Attic R. F. lekythos. Englefield Sale, 40 (Height given there 12½in).

55:61. Three separate drawings of three different vases mounted together: (i) Woman standing before a funerary mound. 'Of the Earl of Elgin. On a whitish ground, the lines of the usual colouring'. 13 x 20.5 cm.

Attic W.-G. (lekythos). JCB: 'The Bird Painter?'.

(ii) Woman with flute-case standing by a palm tree. 'Lord Elgin'. 14.7 x 13.7 cm.

Attic W.-G. (alabastron). DvB: 'Syriskos Painter'.

(iii) Crouching warrior. 11 x 19 cm.

Attic R. F. skyphos, Wisbeach Museum. ARV[2] 559, 148. The Pan Painter. C.M. Robertson JHS lv, 1935 67-70. pl. 8.

56:62. Four separate drawings of three different vases mounted together. (i) Crouching Nike. 'Cover of Greek Patera. Sir H. Englefield'. 12.3 x 17.7 cm.

(ii) Similar to (i). 12.5 x 19.3 cm.

(iii) Infant crawling towards a table, right. 'Mr Graham'. 11 x 17.5 cm.

Attic R. F. chous. Graham Sale, 10 (bought by Dr Clarke) or 12 (bought by Heber). This and the following not illustrated in van Hoorn.

(iv) Infant crawling towards a table, left. 'A Greek Vase in the Collection of the Earl of Elgin'. 11 x 19.2 cm.

Attic R. F. chous.

57:63. Two separate drawings of two different vases mounted together: 24.5 x 41 cm. (i) Prothesis. 'Facsimile of a Greek Vase in the Collection of the Earl of Elgin. Athenian'. Attic W.-G. lekythos. JCB: 'Sabouroff Painter'.

(ii) Bearded man at a blazing altar. 'Facsimile of a Greek Vase in the Collection of the Earl of Elgin. Athenian'.

London D25. Attic W.-G. lekythos.

58:64. Drawing. Oil-seller seated left and standing youth, right. 'A Greek Vase in the Collection of the Earl of Elgin. Athenian. Facsimile. On this figure there can be distinctly seen lines of another different arrangement of folds, indented but without colour'. 23.5 x 41 cm.

Attic W.-G. lekythos. JCB: 'Was once in Aldbourne, then London in the Bomford Collection'.

59:65. Drawing. Youth standing left and woman seated right, at a stele. 'Earl of Elgin. Athenian'. 23 x 28 cm.

Attic W.-G. lekythos. JCB: 'The Reed Painter?'

60:66. Drawing. Left, Eos carrying Memon; right, fight over body of Hektor. 'Opposite sides of a Greek Vase in the Collection of the Earl of Elgin. Found at Girgenti'. 24.5 x 43.8 cm. Louvre CA4201. Attic B. F. neck-amphora. In a letter to the author D. von Bothmer remarks: 'The vase was definitely in Elgin's collection because it was photographed at Broomhall by Lady Beazley and was sold by Lord Elgin to Koutoulakis in the late fifties.' See further, Landes and Laurens, no. 92 for the later history at Béziers. See also Bothmer, p.76, fig. 80; cf. Millingen, pls. 4 and 5. Curiously, Millingen records the vase as being in the possession of William Hamilton Esq., Elgin's former secretary.

61:67. Drawing. Departure of a warrior. 'Earl of Elgin'. 22.3 x 37 cm.
Attic R. F. DvB: 'Perhaps Nolan amphora; the old man on the other side? Achilles Painter?'

62:68. Drawing. Achilles and Penthesilea. 'Earl of Elgin' 19.5 x 30 cm.

Cambridge GR 3. 1971. Attic R. F. calyx-krater. ARV 361, 3. The Pan Painter: Sotheby's 12 July 1971, no. 90 with plate.

62:69. Drawing. Left, bearded man with alabastron; right, woman with a chest; the two divided by a border. 'Greek Lachrymatory. Earl of Elgin. Athenian. Opposite sides'. 19.8 x 27 cm.

Attic R.F. alabastron: DvB: 'Syriskos Painter?'

63:70. Drawing. Scene in a gynaikonitis. 'A Greek Vase in the Collection of the Earl of Elgin. Athenian'. A pyxis is sketched above. Left side of drawing perforated. 23 x 47 cm.

Attic R.F. pyxis. This is the vase referred to by Betton in a letter cited by Jenkins, note 39.

64:71. Drawing. Athena in combat with giant. 'Mr Weber's'. 15.5 x 28 cm.

Attic B. F. Probably lekythos.

64:72. Drawing. Two mounted warriors fighting over one fallen. 'Earl of Elgin.' 24.2 x 35 cm.

Attic B. F. neck-amphora. ABV 284.6. Near the Group of Toronto 305. DvB: 'Sold to Koutoulakis in the late 1950s. Sold by K. to Callimanopoulos in 1982'.

65:73. Drawing. Demeter seated accompanied by gods, and figures bearing torches. 'Athenian vase bought to England by Mr Graham'. 20.8 x 31 cm.

Attic R. F. pelike. Graham Sale, 209 with illus. (Height given here 17½ in). Thence E. D. Clarke. Metzger 34, 2. pl. 14/1 (After Sandford Graham). Metzger quotes Beazley in a letter of 26 March 1957: 'I do not make out the painter, but his is evidently of the high Kerch period contemporary with the Eleusinian pelike and the Marsyas painter. One thinks of the Marsyas painter, but I really cannot say that it is his'.

65:74. Drawing. Departure of warrior. 'Athenian vase brought to England by Mr Graham.' 22 x 29.3 cm. Watermark on mounting sheet: J. Whatman 1840.

Attic R. F. DvB: 'Probably Phiale Painter'. Graham Sale, 206. (Height given there 14½ in). Thence Millingen?

66:75. Drawing. Scene in a gynaikonitis. 'Athenian vase brought to England by Mr Graham.' 23.3 cm x 44.7 cm. Watermark on drawing: J. Whatman 1811, on mounting sheet: J. Whatman 1840.

Attic R. F. DvB: 'This could be from a hydria'. Graham Sale, 208. (Height given there 13½). Thence Latham.

67:76. Drawing. Youth with lyre, left, and youth with torch and staff, right. 'Athenian vase brought to England by Mr Graham'. 20 x 25 cm.

Attic R. F. DvB: 'Should be a skyphos'. Graham Sale, 207. (Height given there 12½). Thence Wilshire.

67:77 Drawing. Youth, left, and woman right, at a stele. 'Athenian vase brought to England by Mr Graham'. 21.7 x 31.7 cm.

Attic W.-G. lekythos. JCB: 'The Reed Painter'. Graham Sale, 191. Thence Latham.

68:78. Drawing. Youth seated at a stele with woman standing left, and youth right. 'Athenian vase brought to England by Mr Graham'. 22 x 28 cm.

Attic W.-G. lekythos. JCB: 'Triglyph Painter'. Probably Graham Sale, 203. (Height given 18½ in). Thence Clarke.

68:79. Drawing. Woman left and youth right at a stele. 'Athenian vase brought to England by Mr Graham.' 21.5 x 27 cm. Watermark on mounting sheet: J. Whatman 1840.

Attic W.-G. lekythos. JCB: 'Reed Painter'. Probably Graham Sale, 30. Thence Combe.

69:80. Drawing. Youth left and woman right at a stele. 'An Athenian vase brought to England by Mr Graham'. 23.5 x 28 cm.

Attic W.-G. lekythos. JCB: 'The Reed Painter'. Graham Sale, 197. (Height given there 18 in). Thence Clarke.

69:81. Drawing. Youth in travelling clothes seated at a stele with standing man left and woman right. 'Athenian vase brought to England by Mr Graham'. 21.5 x 29.5 cm. Watermark on mounting sheet: J. Whatman 1840.

Attic W.-G. lekythos. JCB: 'The Triglyph Painter'. Graham Sale, 48. (Height given there 21 in). Thence Mitchell.

70:82. Two separate drawings mounted side-by-side (i) Drunken satyr. 'A Greek vase in the collection of Richard Westmacott Esq. RA'. 22.5 x 22.5 cm. (ii) Maenad running to right. 22.5 x 15.3 cm.

South-Italian R. F. Two sides of same vase? ADT: 'This vase is not otherwise known to me, and I think there must be addition to the original, especially the strange objects behind the laver'.

71:83. Three separate drawings mounted together. The measurements of the individual drawings are obscured by the overlapping edges. Watermark on mounting sheets: J. Whatman 1840.

(i) Two grooms with horses.

Fragment of Attic B. F. lekythos. Walpole, 322. Plate facing page 325. Brought from Athens by Lord Aberdeen.

(ii) Herakles and Cerberus. 'Mr Gwennap'. Attic B.F. olpe or, possibly, oinochoe. Not found in Brommer, 91-7.

(iii) Four marching warriors with dog. 'Adam Buck'. Attic B.F. lekythos.

72:84. Drawing. Two warriors fighting over a fallen third. Two panthers (on the shoulder). 'Mr Gwennap'. 15 x 19.5 cm.
Attic B. F. lekythos. DvB: 'Should be Phanyllis Group D'. Cf. Haspels, 204, D, 1.

72:85. Engraving. Beazley letter 10. 'Fragment of a Greek vase in the possession of Edward Davenport Esq.' 8.3 x 35.8 cm.
DvB: 'Should be fragments of a B. F. band cup or rim of a B. F. volute krater'.

72:86. Three separate drawings of three different vases mounted together. 9.4 x 42.4 cm overall. Watermark on mounting sheet: J. Whatman 1840.
(i) Huntsman with dog attacking hind. 'The same collection' - i.e. as (ii). Attic B. F. lekythos.
(ii) Two racing-chariots at a winning-post. 'A Greek vase in the Collection of the Earl of Carlisle'.
Attic, Haemonian B. F. lekythos. Carlisle Sale, 3.2.
(iii) Racing chariot at winning-post. 'An Athenian vase in the possession of Adam Buck'.
Attic, Haemonian B. F. lekythos.

73:87. Drawing. Gigantomachy. 'Edward Davenport'. 21 x 32 cm. Watermark on mounting sheet: J. Whatman 1840.
Attic B. F. neck-amphora. This and the following, probably from the same vase.

73:88. Drawing. Two Greek warriors separated from fighting. 'Edward Davenport'. 19.5 x 30 cm.
Attic B. F. neck-amphora.

74:89. Drawing. Athena separating two warriors. 'Earl of Carlisle. Late Henry Tresham'. 19.5 x 26.2 cm.
Attic B. F. Carlisle Sale, 7. (Height given there 12½ in).

74:90. Drawing. Athena in Gigantomachy 'Lord Northwick'. 18.7 x 35.4 cm.
Attic B. F. DvB: 'Athena Painter?'. Possibly Northwick Sale, 1401.

75:91. Three separate drawings of three different vases mounted together. Watermark on mounting sheet: J. Whatman 1840.
(i) Seated gods. 11.5 x 20.5 cm.
Attic B. F. lekythos. DvB: 'Class of Athens 581'.
(ii) Athena between two seated heroes. 'Chinnery'. 14.5 x 34.8 cm.
Attic B. F. lekythos. Chinnery Sale, 105. (Height given there 12 in).
(iii) Dionysos and maenad as symposiasts. 'A Greek Vase in the Collection of Henry Tresham RA.; A Greek Vase in the British Museum'. 11.5 x 15.2 cm. Not seen. DvB: 'Probably a lekythos; cf. ABV 493, 88'.

76:92. Drawing. Satyr seated left, maenad right, separated by an Ionic column. 'A Greek Praefericulum in the possession of John Hinxman Esq.' 22.2 x 30. 8 cm. South-Italian R. F. ADT: 'Campanian. This must be one of the smaller vases of the Ixion Painter, but as yet I have found no record of it'.

77:93. Drawing. Herakles and Geras. 'A Greek Vase in the Collection of the Earl of Elgin'. 28.2 x 36.2 cm. Watermark on drawing. J. Whatman 1811; on mounting sheet, J. Whatman 1840.
Reverse of 62:68.

78: 94 (a). Drawing. Woman seated with youth standing left and woman right. 'Done by Adam Buck from a painting on a Greek Vase in the British Museum'. A reference to the Townley Collection has been deleted. The shape of a pelike is sketched above.

(b) Engraving of same. Inscribed with the artist's initials enclosed within a circle. 22.5 x 31.7 cm. London F181. (Apulian R. F. pelike. RVAp 259, 1. Painter of London Pelikai) Now thought to be Lucanian - Brooklyn Budapest Painter, LCS Suppl. III. 68 listed as BB17.

79: 95 (a) Two separate drawings mounted side-by-side. (i) Two women with castanets. 'A Greek Vase in the possession of Charles Townley'.

(ii) A single woman dancing with castanets. 'A Greek vase in the possession of Charles Townley'. The shape of a pelike is sketched in the top left-hand corner. 20.8 x 42.5 cm (for the two).

80:95 (b) Engraving of same. Beazley letter 7. Inscribed with the artist's initials enclosed within a circle. 20.2 x 40.5 cm.

London E357, (two sides). Attic R.F. pelike. ARV^2 555, 94. The Pan Painter.

81:96 (a). Drawing. Youth right leaning on a stele, woman left. 'British Museum. Late Townley'. 29 x 26 cm.

81:96 (b). Engraving of same. Inscription erased but appears to refer in the usual formula to Townley as the owner. 20 x 25.2 cm.

London F98. Apulian hydria. RVAp 290, 22. Close to the Zaandam Group.

82:97 (a). Drawing. Woman seated left, warrior standing right. 'British Museum. Late Townley. From the Gorio Collection. Bell'. 20 x 26.7 cm.

82:97 (b). Engraving of same. No inscription. 21.5 x 23 cm.

London F. 191. Campanian bell-krater. LCS 485, 324. The CA Painter.

83:98. Drawing. Judgement of Paris. 'British Museum. Late Townley. Bell. Engraved in Mus. Pio. Clem.' 25 x 39.7 cm.

London F167. Apulian bell-krater. RVAp 263, 26. Judgement Painter.

84:99. Drawing. Herakles and centaur left, Athena right. 'British Museum. Late Townley. From Gorio Collection'. 23.5 x 32 cm.

London F43. Apulian bell-krater.

84:100. Drawing. Eos and Kephalos, old man standing right. 'Richard Payne Knight. Bell'. 23 x 34.5 cm. London E320 (two sides). Attic R. F. amphora. ARV^2 989, 32. The Achilles Painter.

85: 101 (a). Drawing. Woman seated centre with youth left, standing woman right holding parasol. 'Richard Payne Knight. 3 Handle'. 22.5 x 30.5 cm.

101 (b). Engraving of same. Inscribed with the artist's initials enclosed within a circle. 22.5 x 30 cm. London F94. Apulian R. F. hydria. RVAp 52, 58. Tarporley Painter.

86:102. Drawing,. Youth seated centre, standing woman with parasol left, standing youth right. 'Rich. Payne Knight. Bell'. 23 x 33 cm.

London F96. Apulian R. F. hydria. RVAp 260, 16. Rehearsal Painter.

86.103. Drawing. Woman seated left, youth standing right. 'Now in the Museum. Richard Payne Knight'. 22.3 x 34.7 cm.

London F463 Apulian R. F. patera. RVAp 589, 281. The Painter of Louvre MNB 1148.

87:104. Engraving. Scene in a gynaikonitis. 'British Museum'. 20.2 x 35 cm.

London E403 (Payne Knight) Attic R. F. pelike. ARV^2 735, 110. The Carlsruhe Painter.

88:105 (a). Drawing. Sack of Troy. 'A Greek Vase in the Collection of Richard Payne Knight Esq. Now in the Museum. From the Albergotti Collection'. 27 x 46 cm.

89:105 (b). Engraving of same. Inscribed with artist's initials enclosed within a circle. 28 x 48 cm.
London F209. Campanian hydria. LCS 433, 538. Very close to the Danaid Painter.

90:106. Three separate drawings mounted side-by-side. 'British Museum'. 20 x 41 cm (overall).
(i) Left. Youth seated.
(ii) Youth left, woman right. London F146 (probably Hamilton Collection). Campanian amphora. LCS App 1, 37.
(iii) Youth leaning on staff. London E290 (Hamilton Collection). Attic R. F. amphora ARV^2 653, 1. The Charmides Painter.

91:107. Drawing. Woman standing left, woman seated right. 'British Museum'. 21.2 x 26 cm.
London E386 (Hamilton Collection). Attic R. F. pelike. ARV^2 735, 112. The Carlsruhe Painter.

91:108. Drawing. Hoplitodromos. 'British Museum'. 23.8 x 29 cm.
London E483. (Ex-Townley). Attic R. F. column-krater.

92:109. Two separate drawings mounted together. (i) Eros and hetairai. (ii) Youths and hetairai. 'British Museum'. 33.8 x 44 cm (for the two).
London F309. (Probably Hamilton Collection). Apulian R. F. pelike RVAp 517, 184. Close to the Egnazia Group.

93:110. Drawing. Woman seated centre, woman left, youth right. Above, woman seated, Eros. 'A Greek Vase in the British Museum'. 29 x 39.5 cm.
Reverse of 92:109.

94: 111 (a). Two Amazons. 'British Museum'. 25 x 27 cm.
111 (b) Engraving of same. Inscribed with the artist's initials enclosed within a circle. 24 x 25.5 cm.
London E295. (Probably Hamilton Collection). Attic R. F. amphora ARV^2 654, 3. Related to the Charmides Painter.

95:112. Two separate drawings of two different vases mounted side-by-side. Inscribed across the two: 'British Museum. Late Townley'. 18.8 x 42.2 cm.
(i) Female entertainer doing a handstand. London F232. Attic R. F. hydria. LCS 375, 112. The Foundling Group.
(ii) Winged female with chest.
London E616. (Probably Hamilton Collection). Attic R.F. lekythos. ARV^2 697, 26. The Icarus Painter.

96: 113 (a). Drawing. Youth with lyre seated left, youth standing right. 'British Museum'. 22 x 23 cm.
113 (b). Engraving of same. No inscription. 19.2 x 21.5 cm.
London E317. (Hamilton Collection). Attic R. F. amphora ARV^2 856, 1. The Painter of London E317.

97:114. Drawing. Youthful warrior seated in naiskos, woman standing left, youth right. 'Greek Vase in the British Museum'. 27.5 x 37 cm.
F334. (Hamilton Collection). Apulian R. F. amphora. RVAp 740, 101. The Patera Painter.

98:115. Drawing. Youthful warrior standing in naiskos; youth standing, woman seated left; woman seated, youth standing right. 'A Greek Vase in the British Museum'. 28.5 x 41.5 cm.
London F282 (Hamilton Collection). Apulian R.F. volute-krater. RVAp 341, 27. The Varrese Painter.

99:116.(i). Drawing. Female head in floral ornament. 'Neck of Vase'. 13 x 34.5 cm. Shoulder of 97:114.
(ii) Similar. 14 x 34.7.
Neck of 98:115.

100:117. Drawing. Stele with youth seated, woman standing left; woman seated, youth standing right. 'British Museum'. 20 x 31.2 cm.
Reverse of 98:115.

100:118. Drawing. Warrior left, woman right. 'British Museum'. 21.5 x 31.2 cm.
London F525. (Probably Hamilton Collection). Campanian R. F. hydria.

101:119. Drawing. Woman left, and two youths. 'British Museum'. 22.8 x 33.5 cm. Watermark on mounting sheet: J. Whatman 1840. Not seen.

101:120. Drawing. Athena left, Herakles right. 'British Museum'. 22 x 30.2 cm. Watermark on mounting sheet: J. Whatman 1840.
London E321. (Probably Hamilton Collection). Attic R.F. amphora. ARV^2 670, 10. Manner of the Painter of London E342.

102:121. Drawing. Woman centre, and two youths. 'British Museum'. 23 x 22 cm.
London F298. (Hamilton Collection). Apulian R. F. column-krater. RVAp 567, 50. The Haifa Painter.

102:122. Drawing. Woman (left) and youth (right) flanking a large funerary vase. 'British Museum'. 24 x 30 cm.
London F336. (Hamilton Collection). Apulian R. F. amphora. RVAp 375, 122. Painter of BM F336.

103:123. Drawing. Offerings at a funerary stele. 'British Museum'. 30.3 x 47.5 cm.
London F213. (Hamilton Collection). Campanian R. F. hydria. LCS 407, 311. The Libation Painter.

104:124. Drawing. Orestes and Apollo. 'British Museum'. 23.2 x 31.7 cm.
London F166. (Hamilton Collection). Apulian R. F. bell-krater RVAp 97, 232. Eumenides Painter.

104:125. Drawing. Woman standing left, youth seated right. 'British Museum'. 20.5 x 29.7 cm.
London F67. (Almost certainly Hamilton Collection). Apulian R. F. bell-krater. RVAp 78, 85. Eton Nika Painter.

105:126. Drawing. Youth pursuing a woman; old man with sceptre looking on. 'British Museum'. 21.5 x 33 cm.
London E198. (Hamilton Collection). Attic R. F. hyrdia ARV^2 606, 79. The Niobid Painter.

105:127. Drawing. Woman standing left, youthful warrior seated right. 'British Museum'. 21.5 x 31 cm.
London F297. (Hamilton Collection). Apulian R. F. column-krater. RVAp 357, 197. The Wolfenbüttel Painter.

106:128. Drawing. Greek, right, fighting Amazons, left. 'British Museum'. 21.5 x 32.7 cm.
London E247. (Hamilton Collection). Attic R. F. hydria. ARV^2 1471, 4. Near Group G.

106:129. Drawing. Woman (left) and youth (right), on either side of stele. 'British Museum'. 18.5 x 23. 5 cm.
Reverse of London F269. (Hamilton Collection). Apulian R. F. calyx-krater. RVAp 339. 11. The Varrese Painter.

107:130. Drawing. Old man seated centre, woman standing left, woman seated right. 'British Museum'. 18.5 x 23.5 cm.
London E211. (Hamilton Collection). Attic R. F. hydria. ARV^2 520, 37. The Syracuse Painter.

107:131. Drawing. Youth pursuing a woman. 'British Museum'. 20 x 27.7 cm.
London E332. (Hamilton Collection). Attic R. F. amphora. ARV^2 1161, 6. The Painter of Munich 2335.

108:132. Drawing. Herakles (?) with Nike, the Dioskouroi (?) and Athena. 'British Museum'. 23.8 x 39.7 cm. Watermark on drawing. J. Whatman 1811.
London E498. (Probably Hamilton Collection). Attic R. F. bell-krater. ARV^2 1334, 16. The Nikias Painter.

109:133 (a) Drawing. Youth with discus left, paidotribes right. 'British Museum'. 20.8 x 28 cm.
(b). Engraving of same. Inscribed with the artist's initials enclosed within a circle. 21.7 x 25.4 cm.
London E395. (Probably Hamilton Collection). Attic R. F. pelike. ARV^2 1140, 1. The Painter of London E395.

110:134. Drawing. Herakles seated with Athena, Eros, and a woman; youth seated with woman standing. 'British Museum'. 20.8 x 24.7 cm.
London F74. (Probably Hamilton Collection). Attic R. F. bell-krater. ARV^2 1448, 5. The Toya Painter.

111:135 (a). Drawing. Nike pursuing a bird. 'British Museum'. 20.8 x 24.7 cm.
(b) Engraving of same. No inscription. 20.2 x 24 cm.
London E538. (Hamilton Collection). Attic R. F. oinochoe. ARV^2 652, 37. The Nikon Painter.

112:136. Drawing. Two youthful symposiasts with two hetairai. 'British Museum'. 21 x 33.3 cm.
London F103. (Hamilton Collection). Campanian R. F. oinochoe. LCS 482, 303. LNO Painter.

112:137. Drawing. Athena driving quadriga. 'British Museum'. 21.3 x 29.5 cm.
London B258. (Hamilton Collection). Attic B. F. amphora. ABV 402, 9. The Group of Würzburg 221.

113:138. Drawing. Two draped youths and three funerary vases. No inscription. 19 x 23.7 cm. Reverse of 113:139.

113:139 Drawing. Departing warrior centre, woman left, woman right.
London F490. (Townley Collection). Campanian column-krater. LCS Appendix I, 60. The Owl Pillar Group.

114:140. Drawing. Two female heads. 'On a small Greek vessel in the Collection of Samuel Rogers Esq.' 18.3 x 8.7 cm. Watermark on drawing: J. Whatman 1811.
Probably from an Attic R. F. askos.

114:141. Drawing. Woman left with alabastron, woman right with fillet. 'British Museum. With two heads from the Rogers Collection'. 21.3 x 22.5 cm.
London E327. Attic R. F. amphora. ARV^2 668, 27. The Painter of London E342.

114:142. Drawing. Two female heads. 'On opposite sides of a Greek Vase in the collection of Charles Townley Esq.' 17.4 x 28.5 cm.
London F496. Campanian bell-krater. LCS 572, 1023. The Vitulazio Painter.

115:143. Drawing. Female head. 'A Greek vase in the Collection of William Danby Esq.' 29.2 x 14.2 cm. Watermark on drawing: J. Whatman 1811. The sheet also features two series of calculations relating to the number of plates engraved under the headings vol. 1, vol. 2.

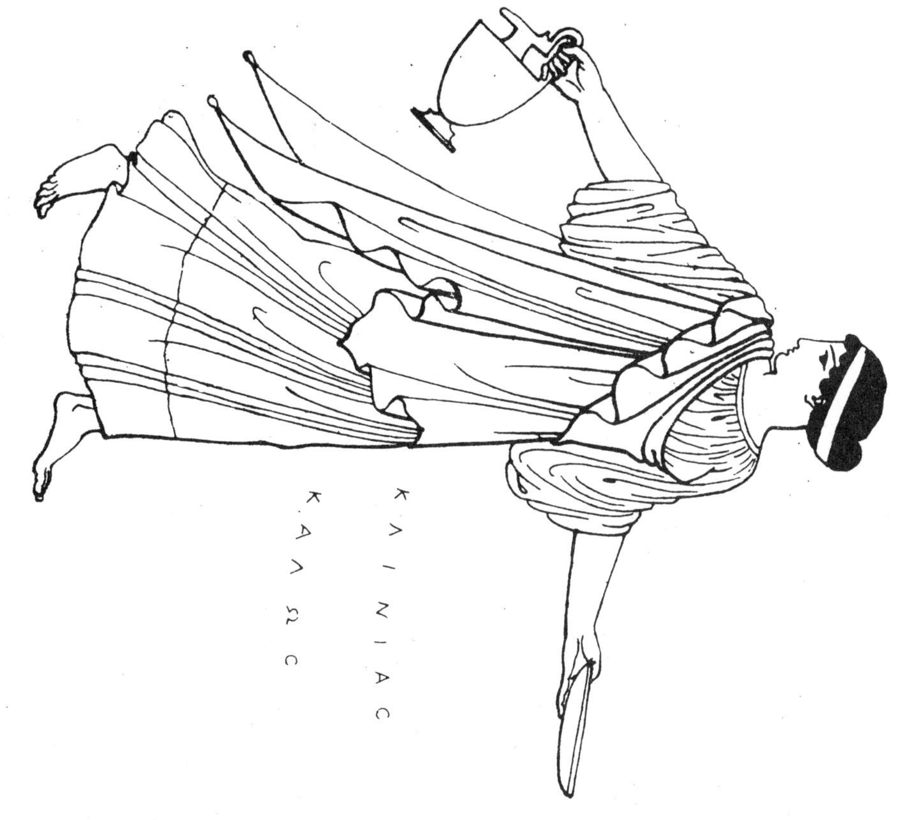
ΚΛΙΝΙΑC
ΚΑΛΩC

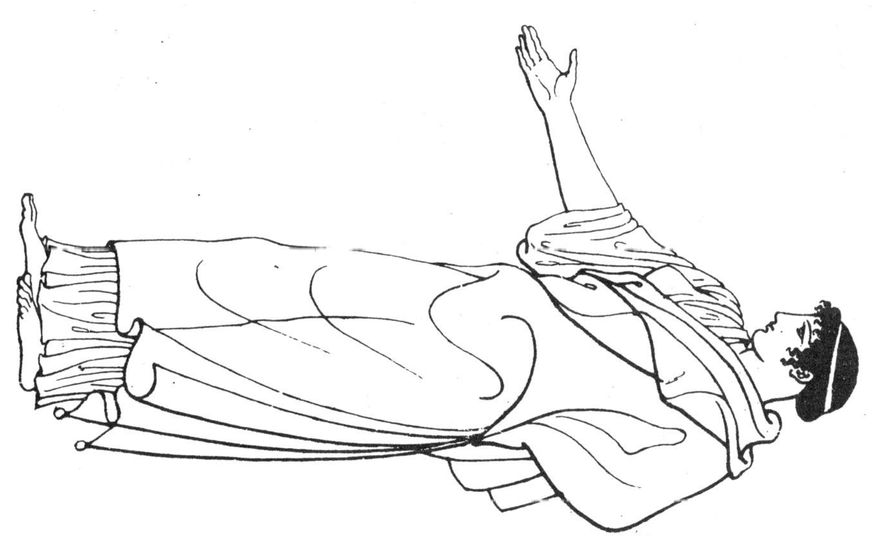

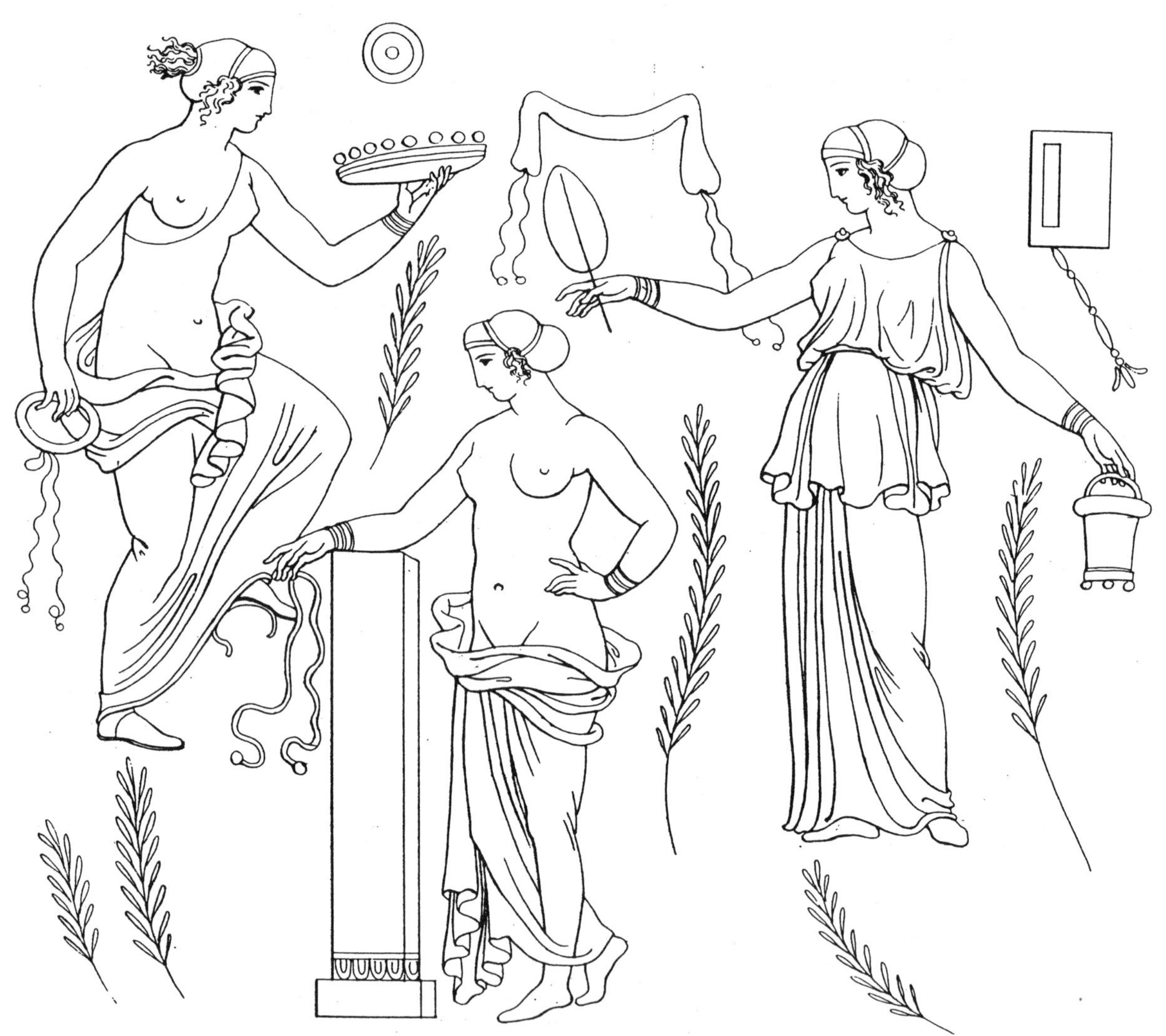

4:3

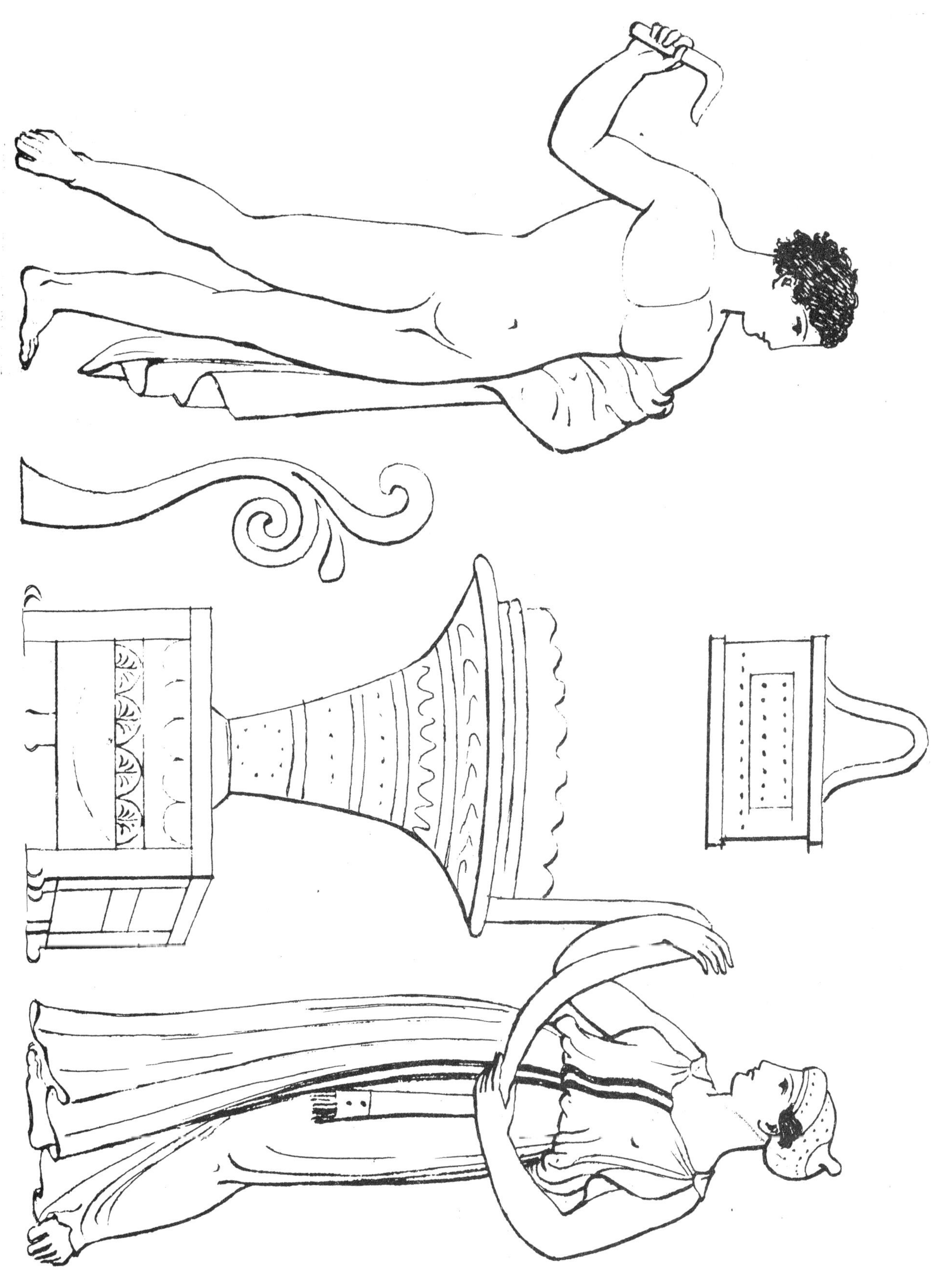

4:4

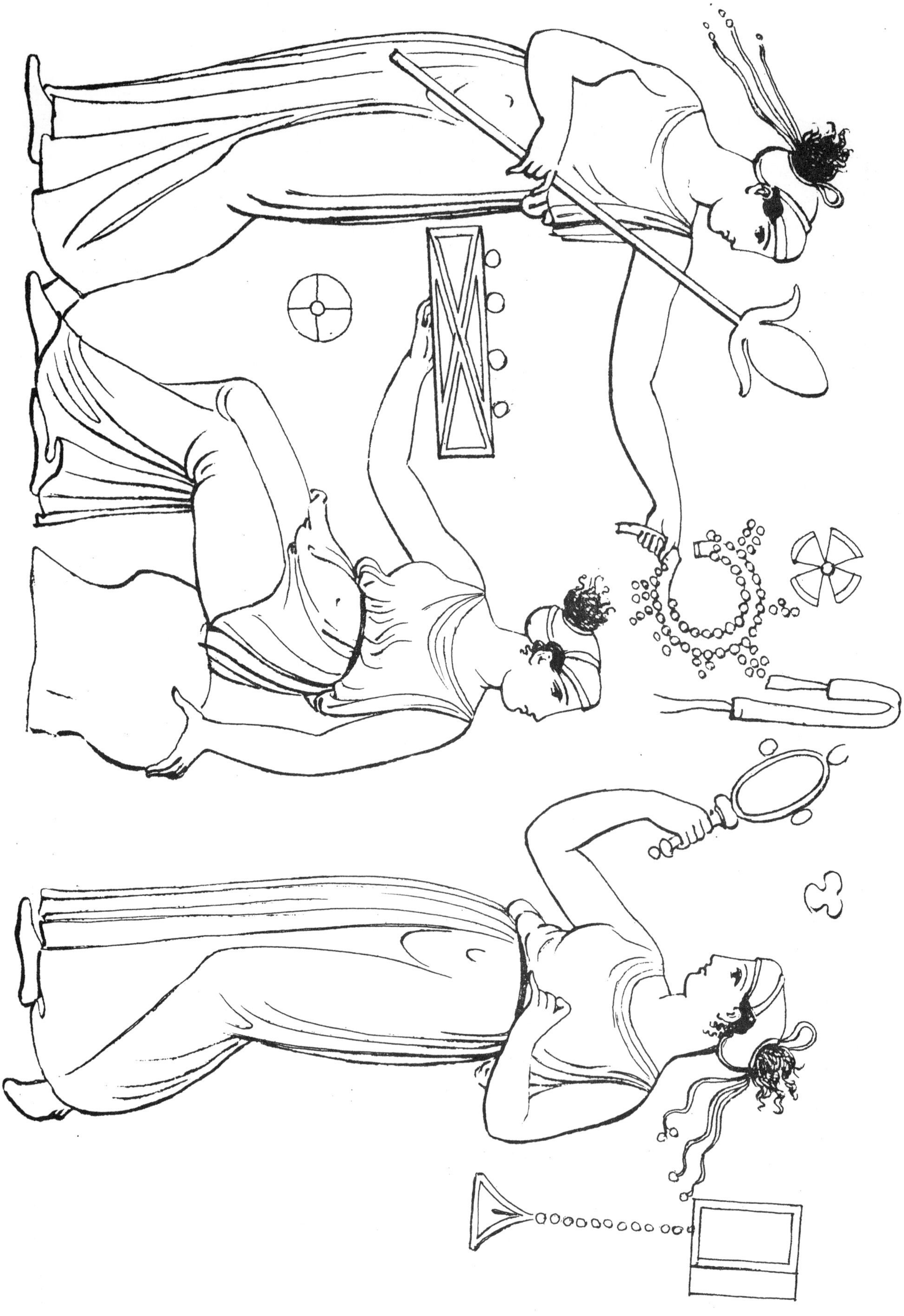

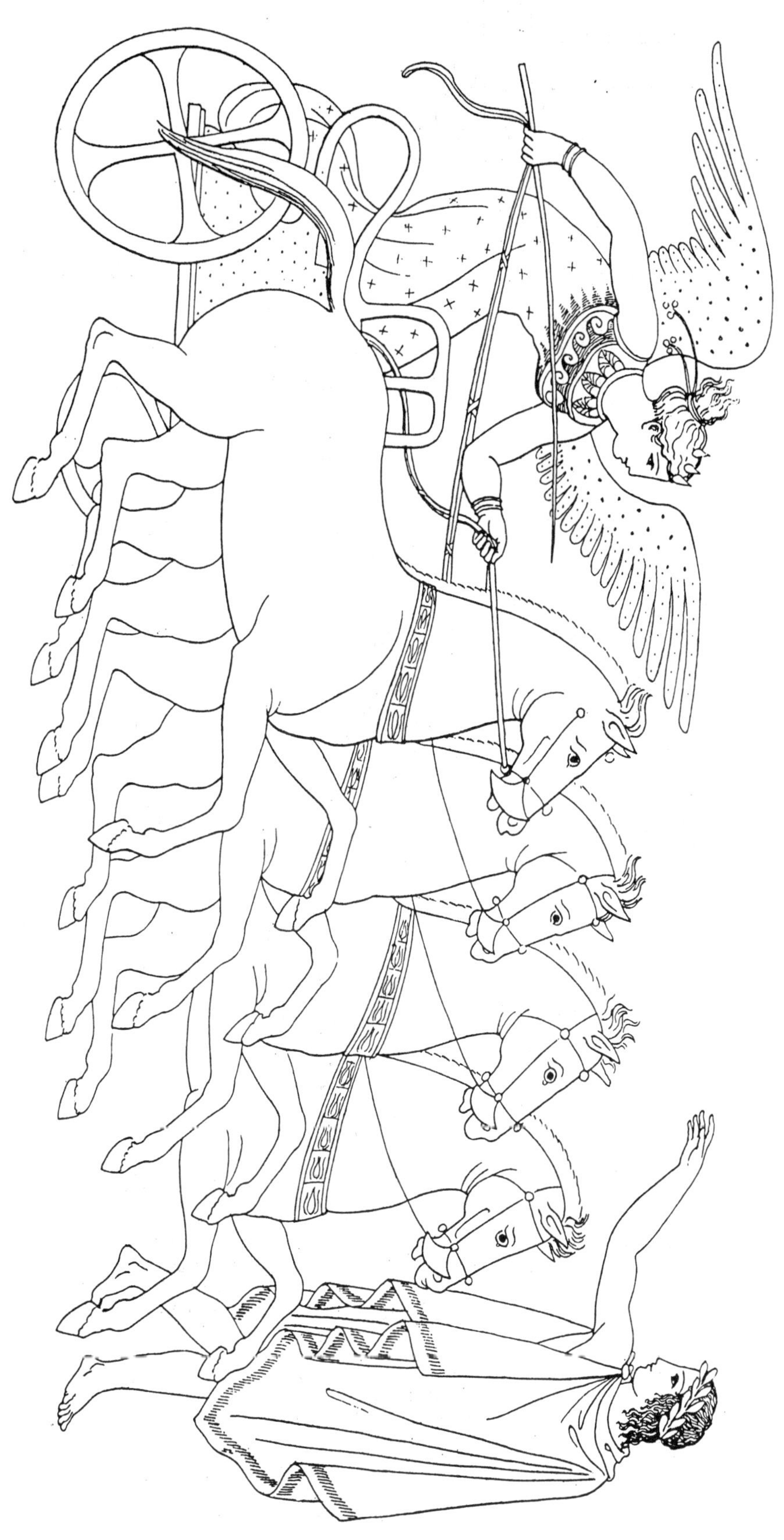

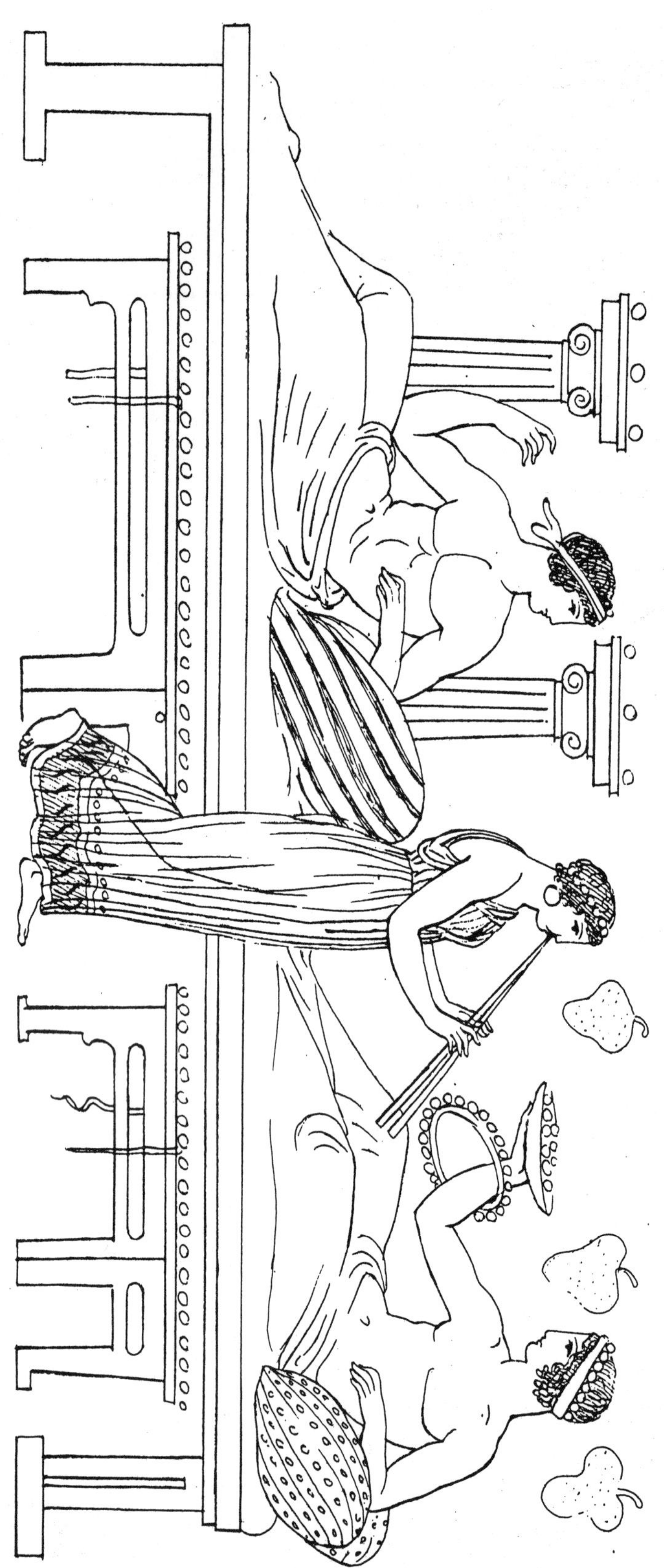

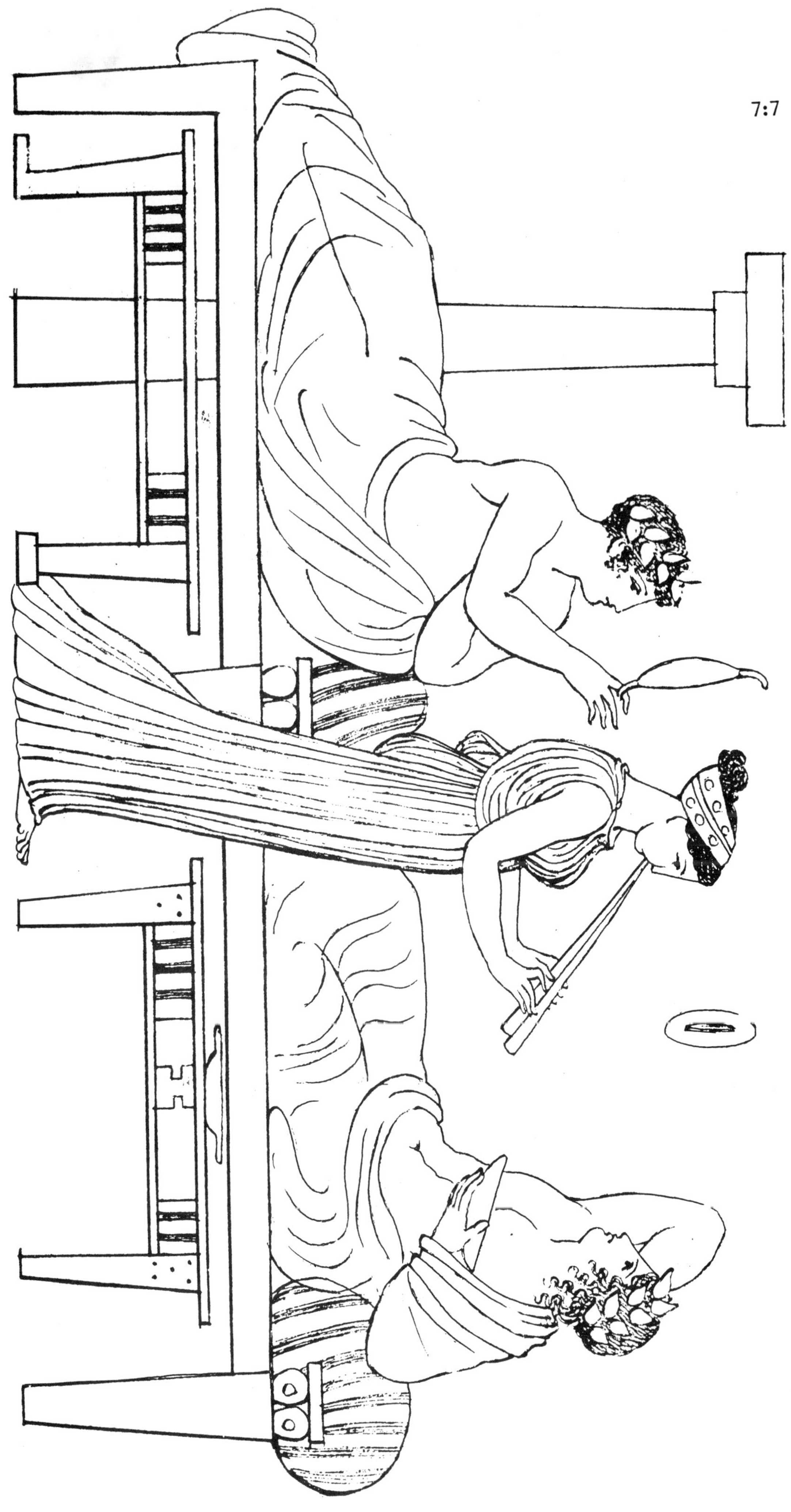

7:7

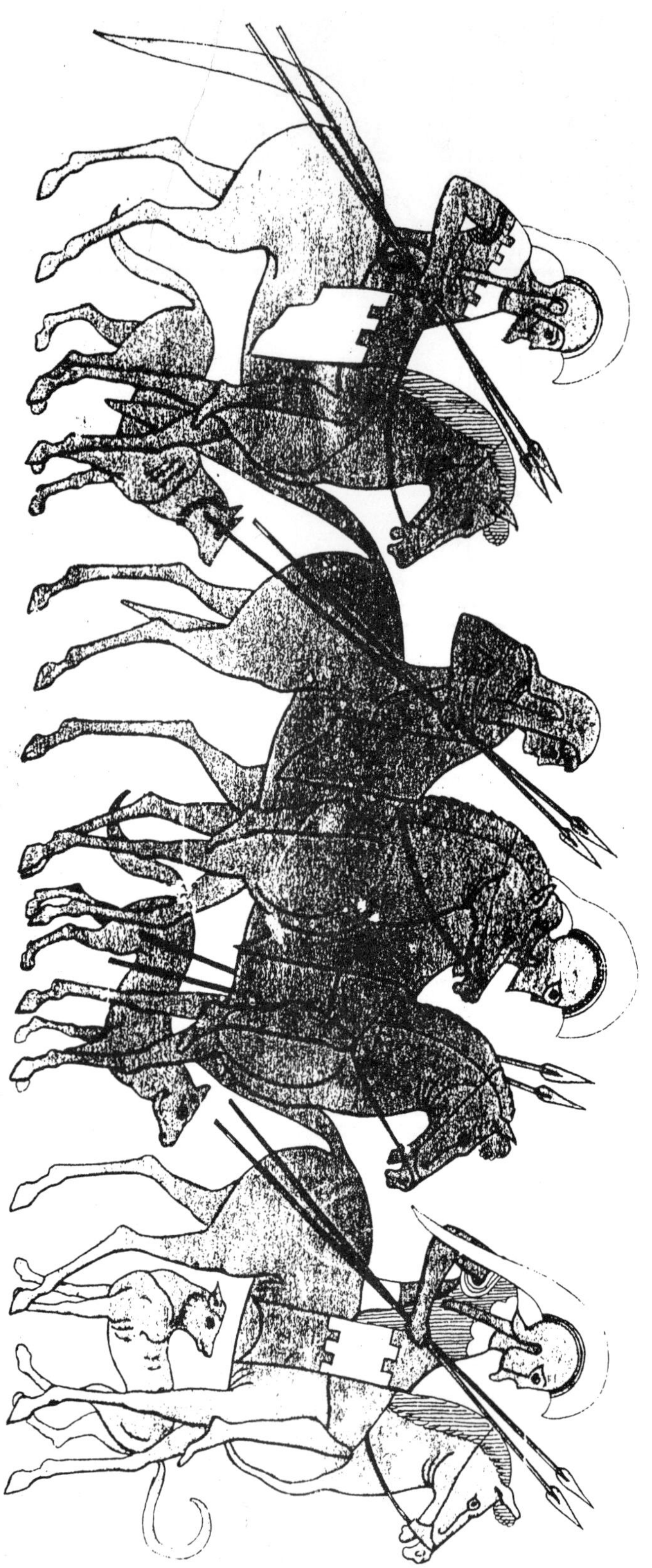

10:9(b)

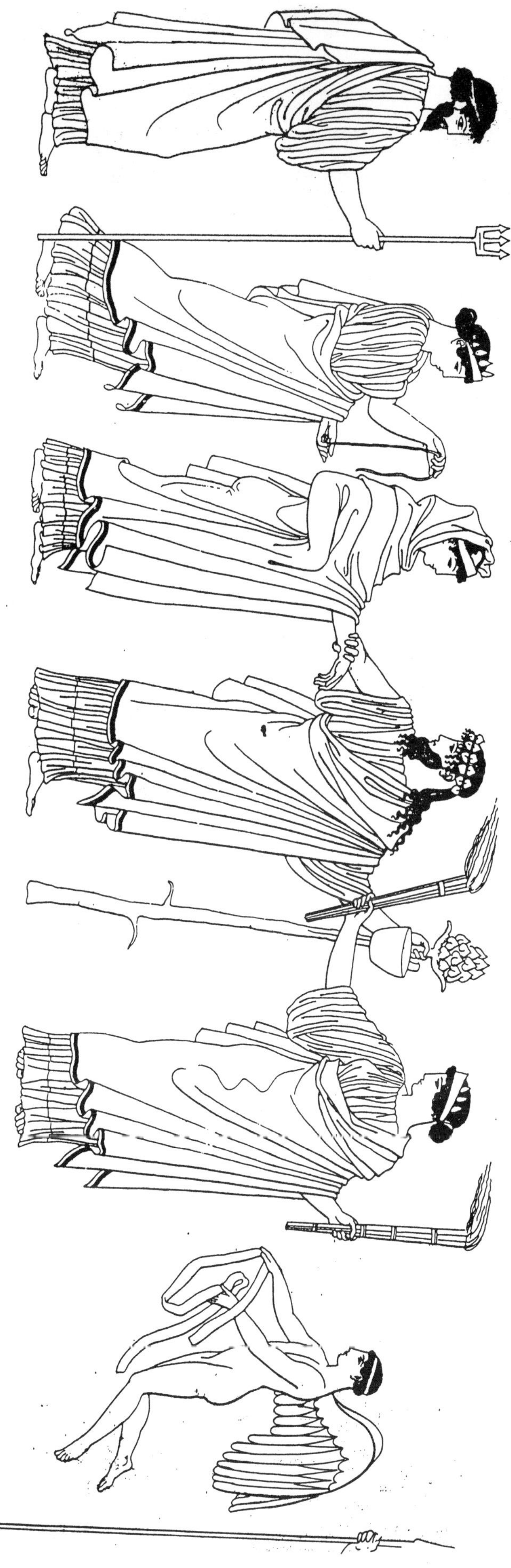

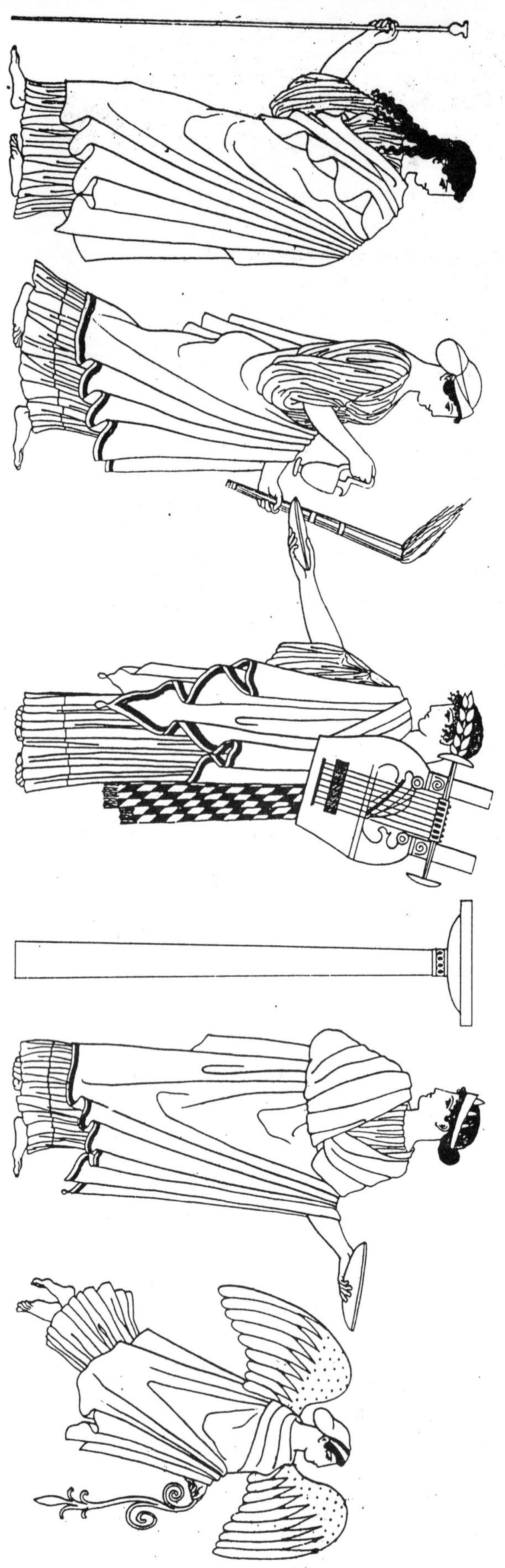

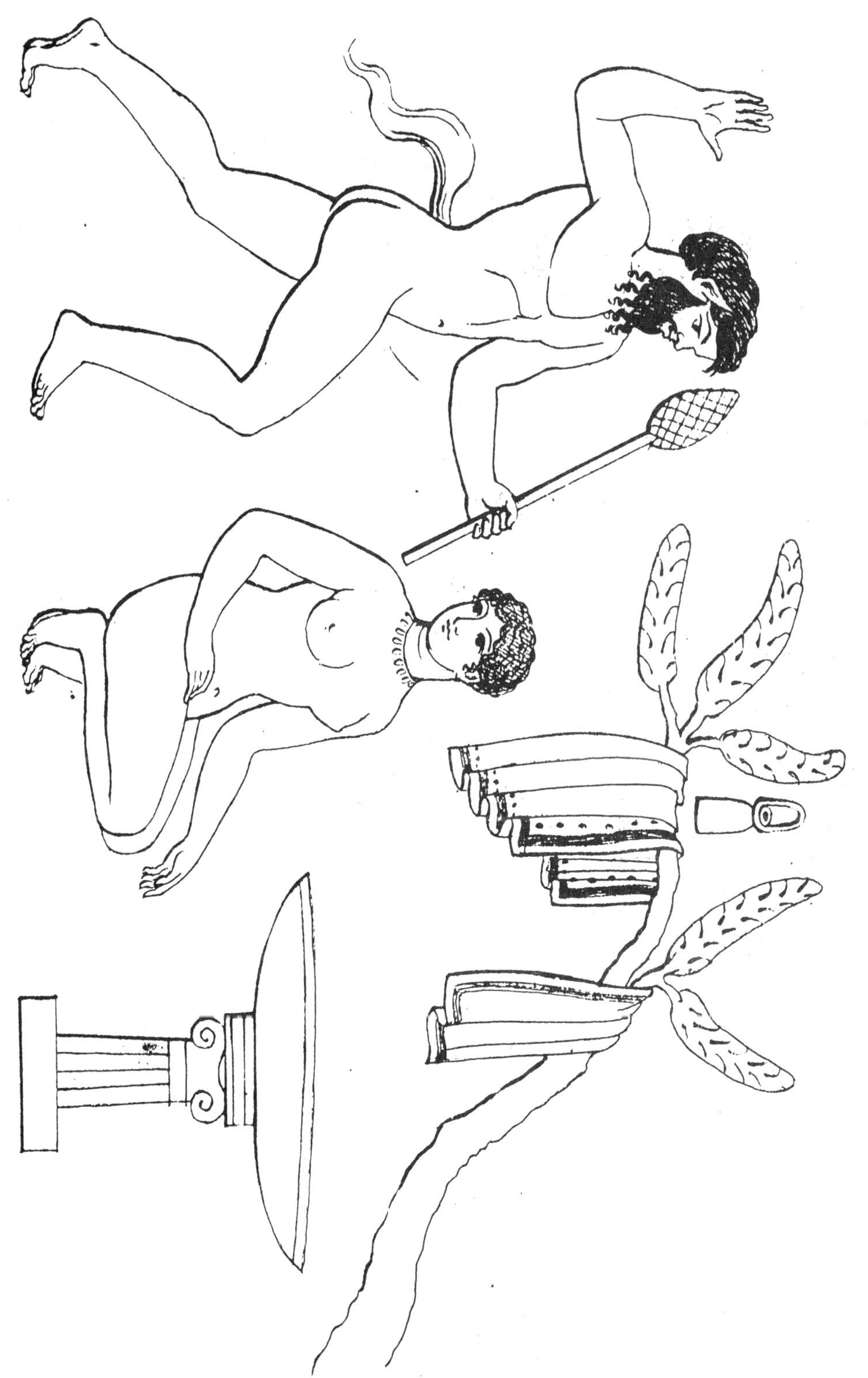

14:12(b)

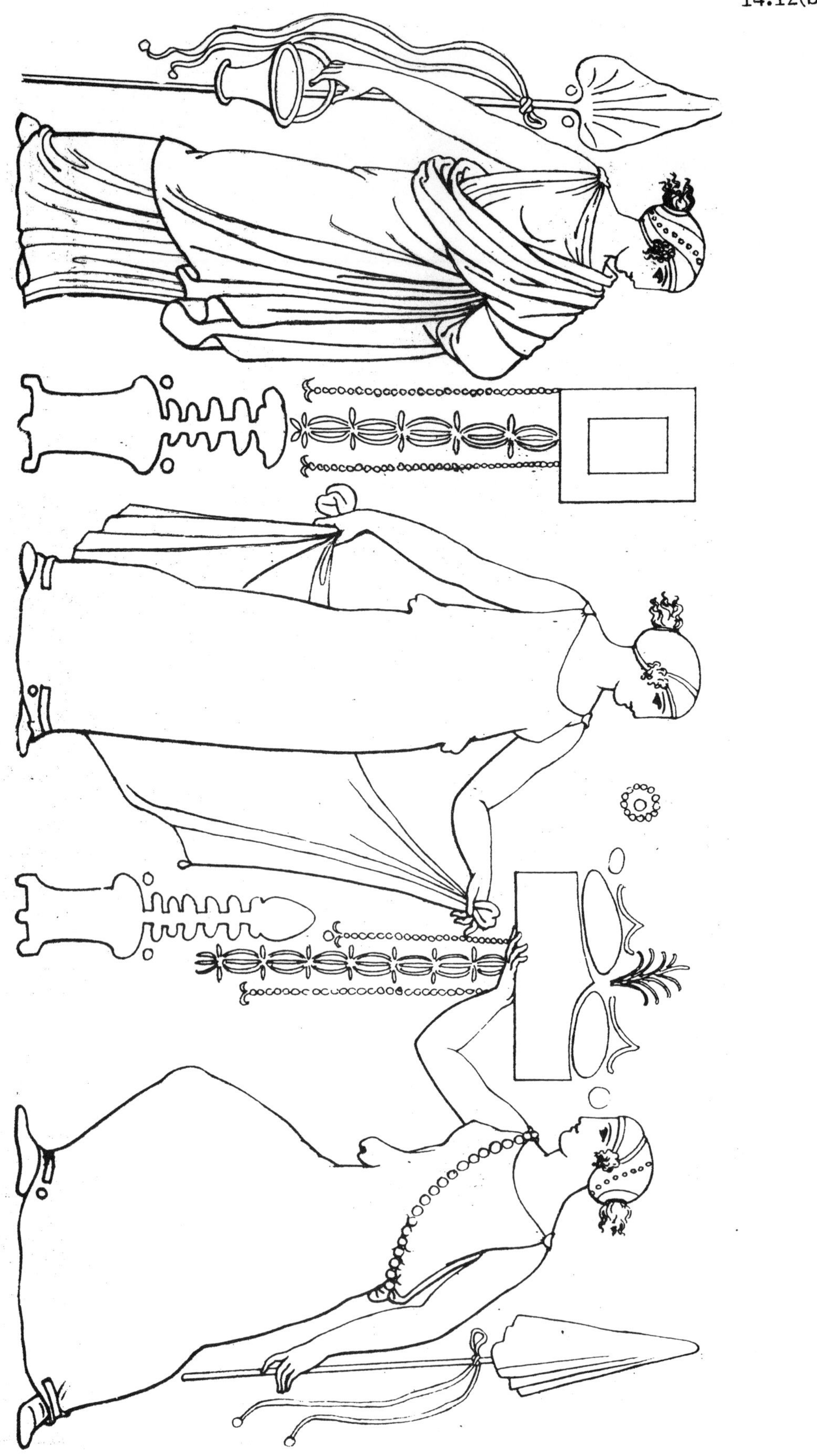

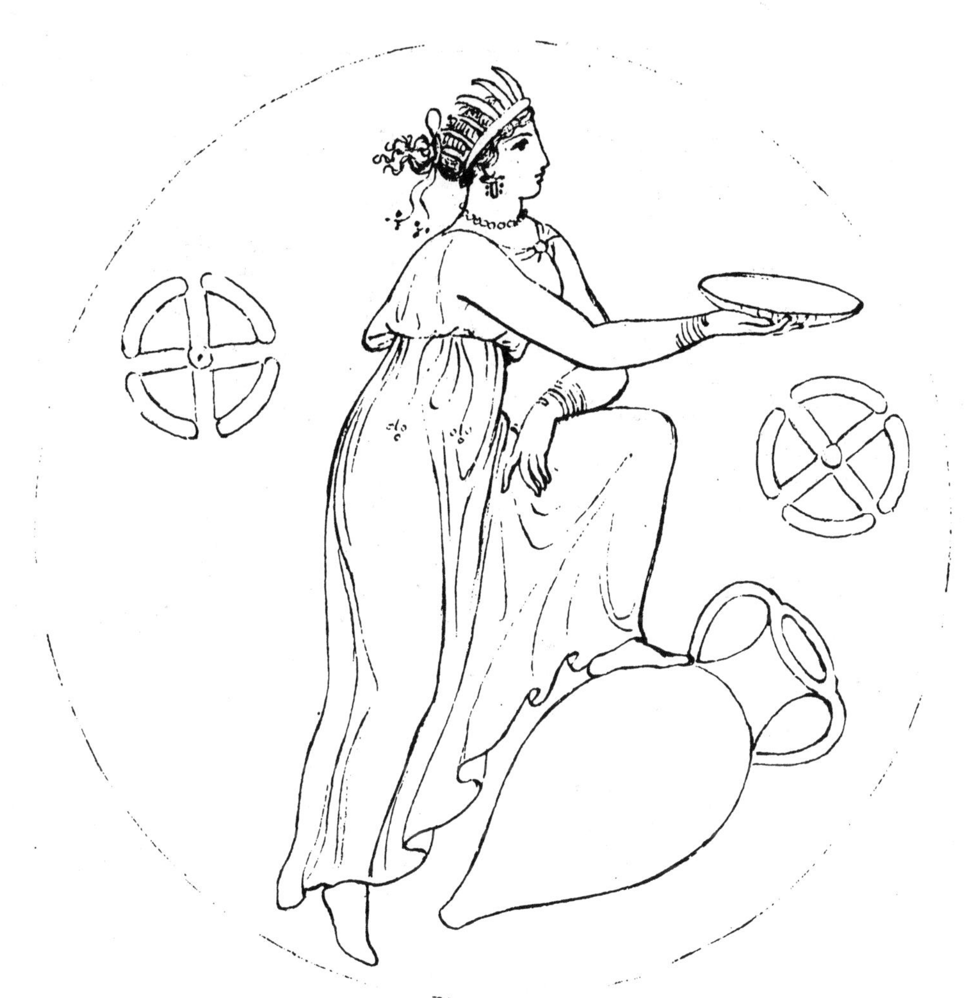

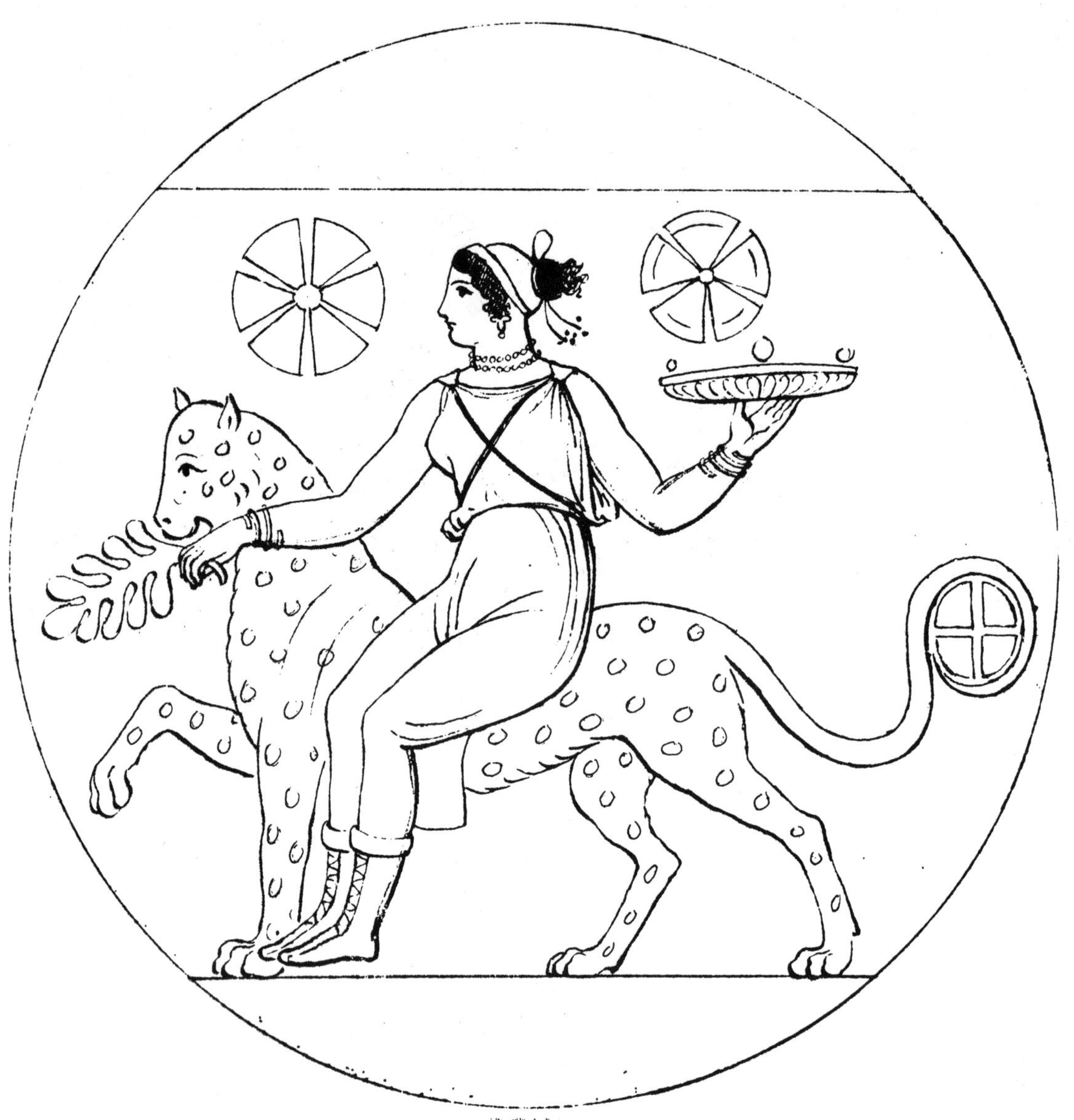

17:16

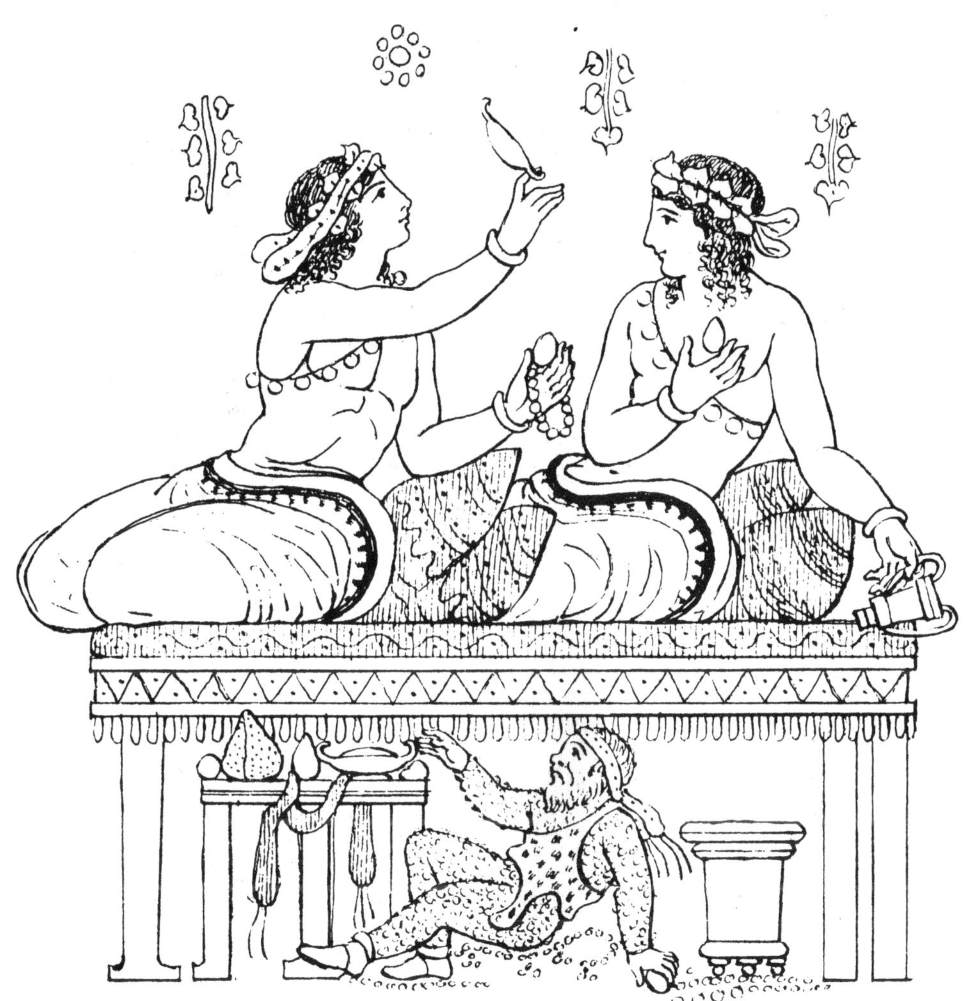

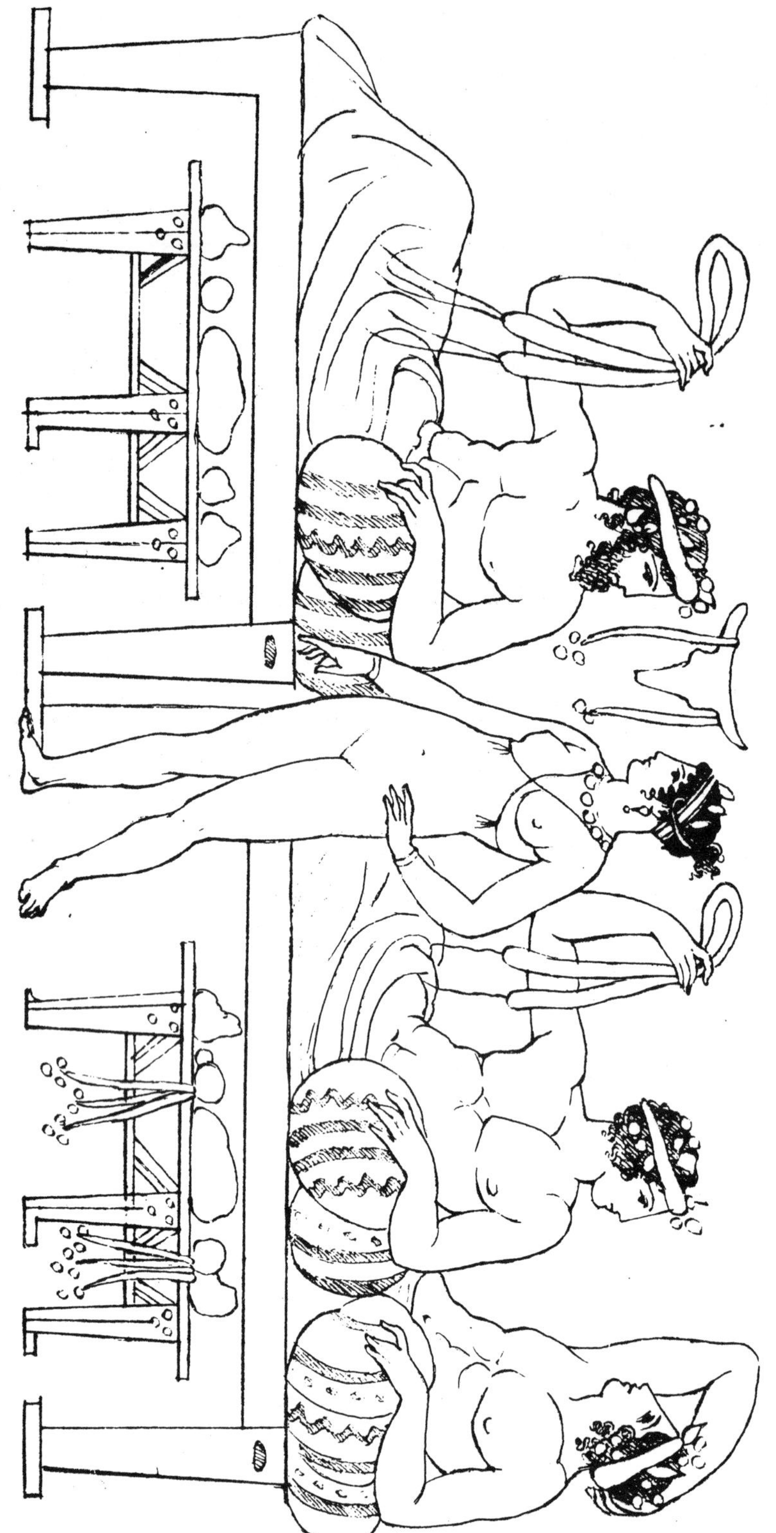

19:20

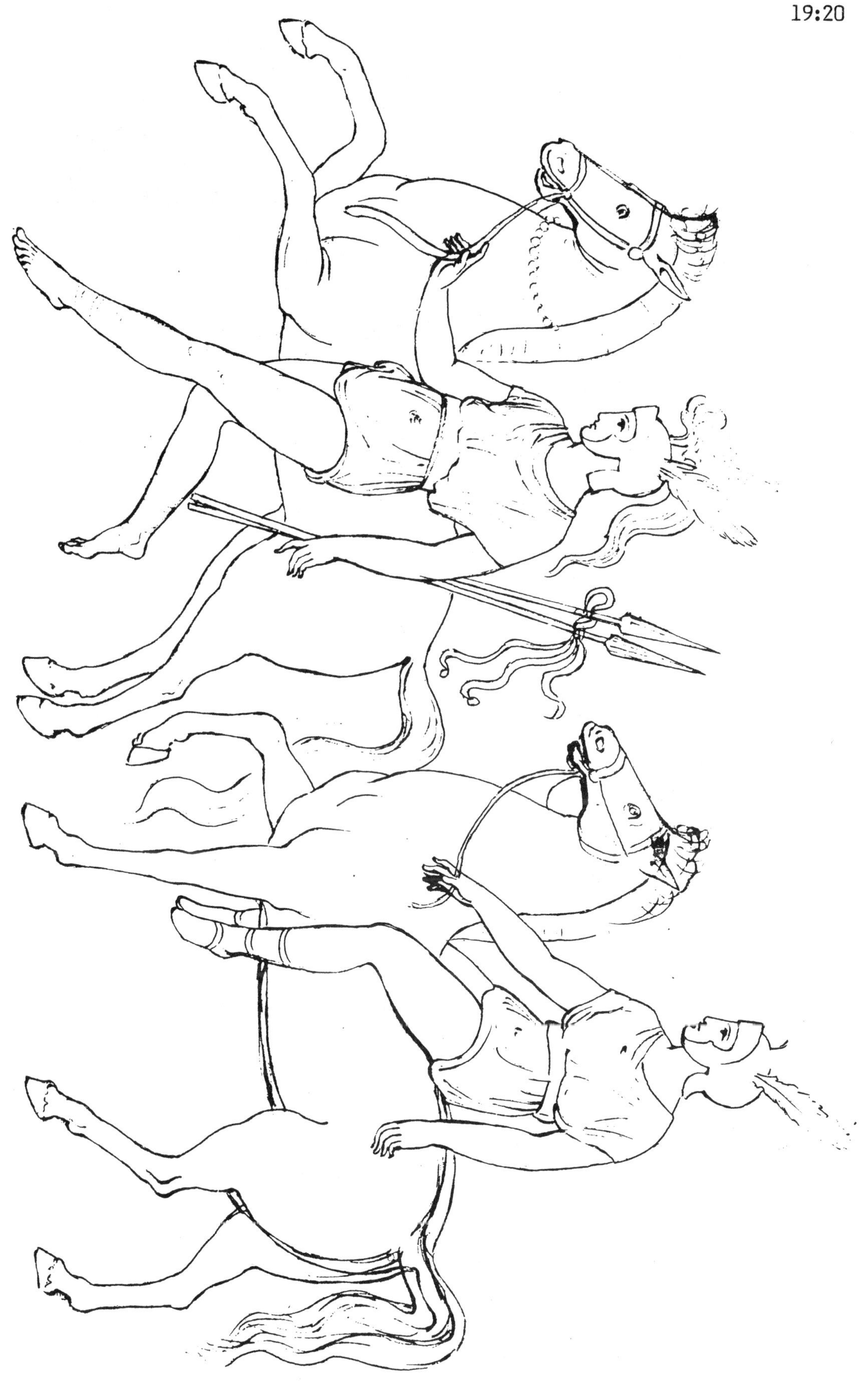

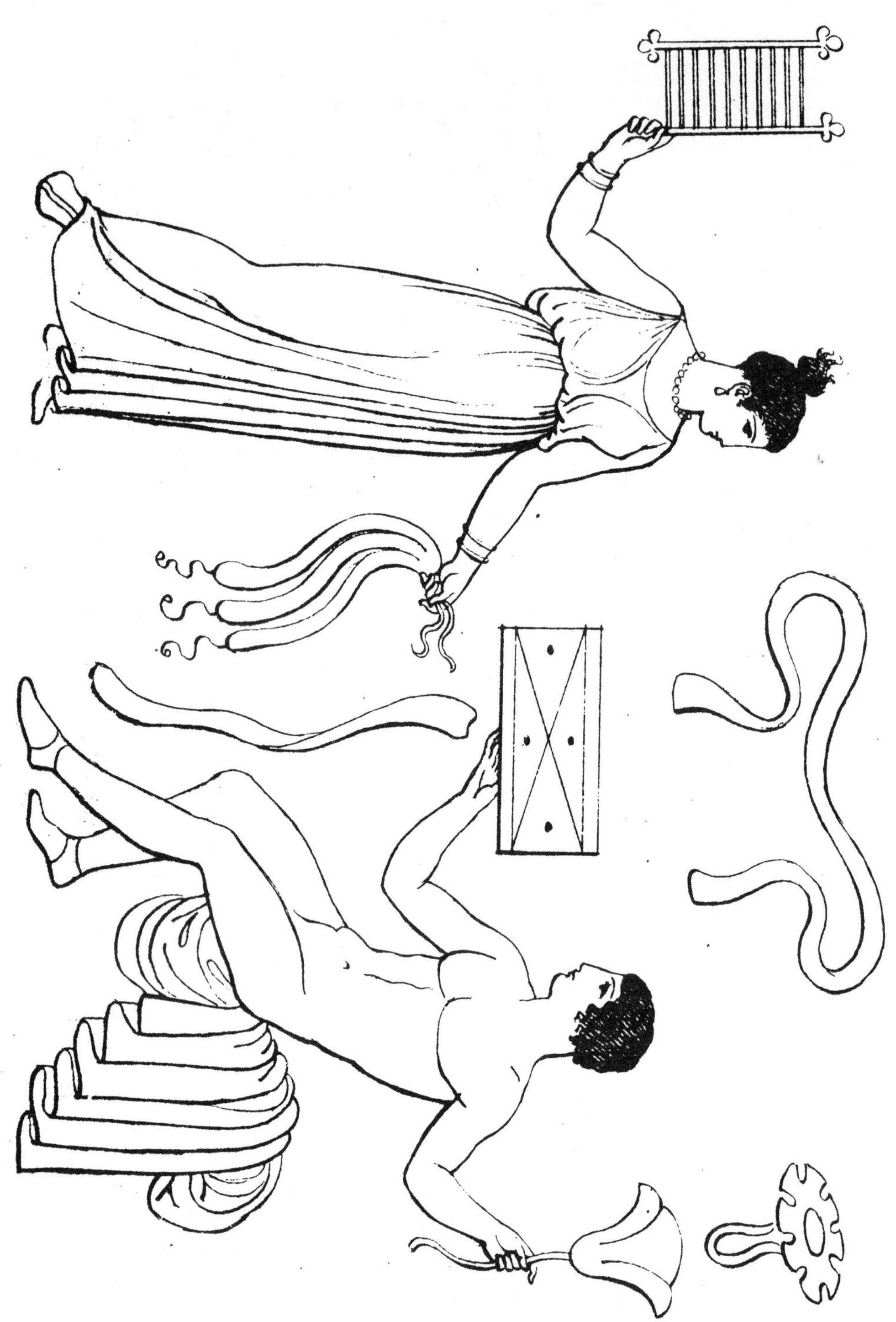

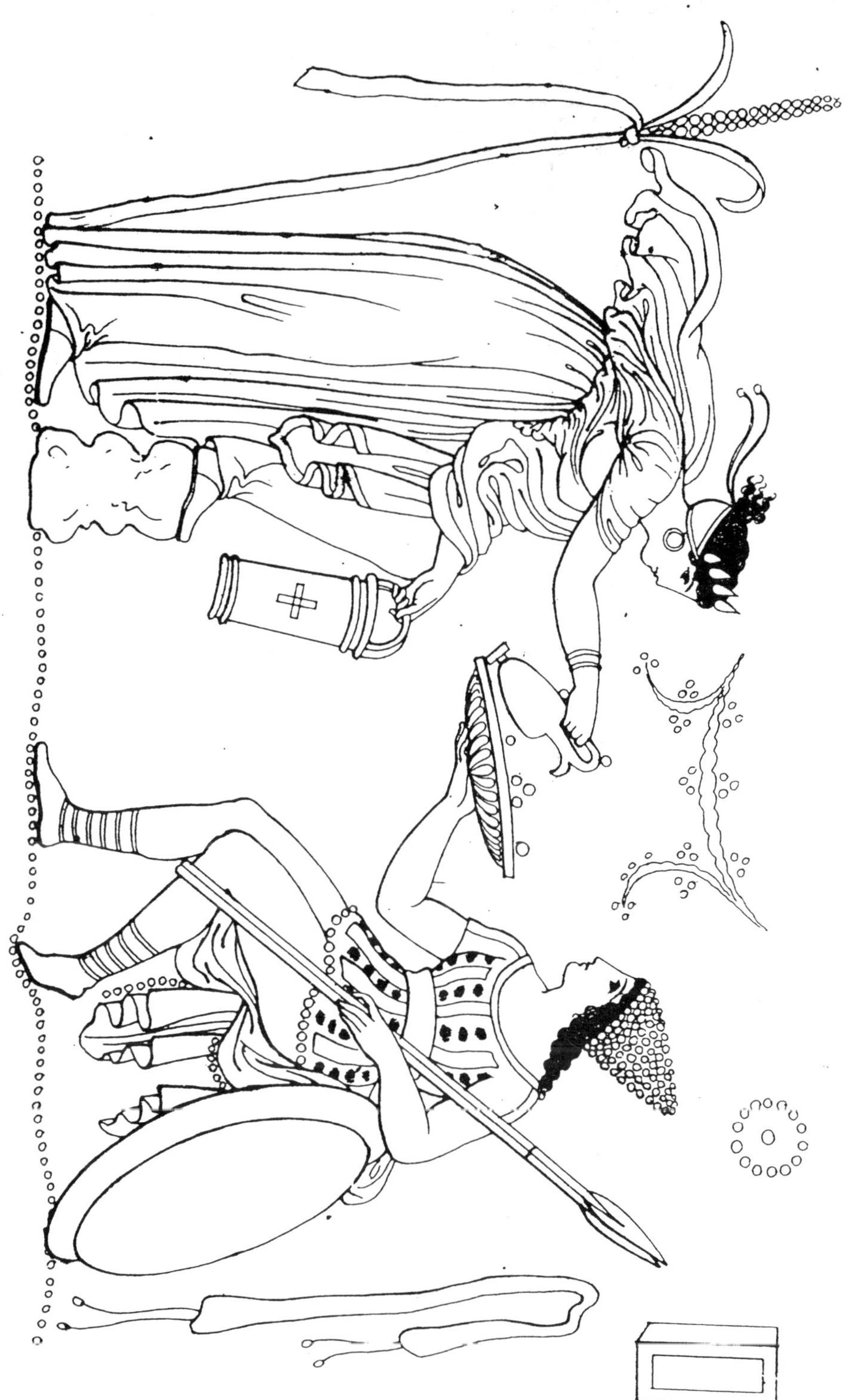

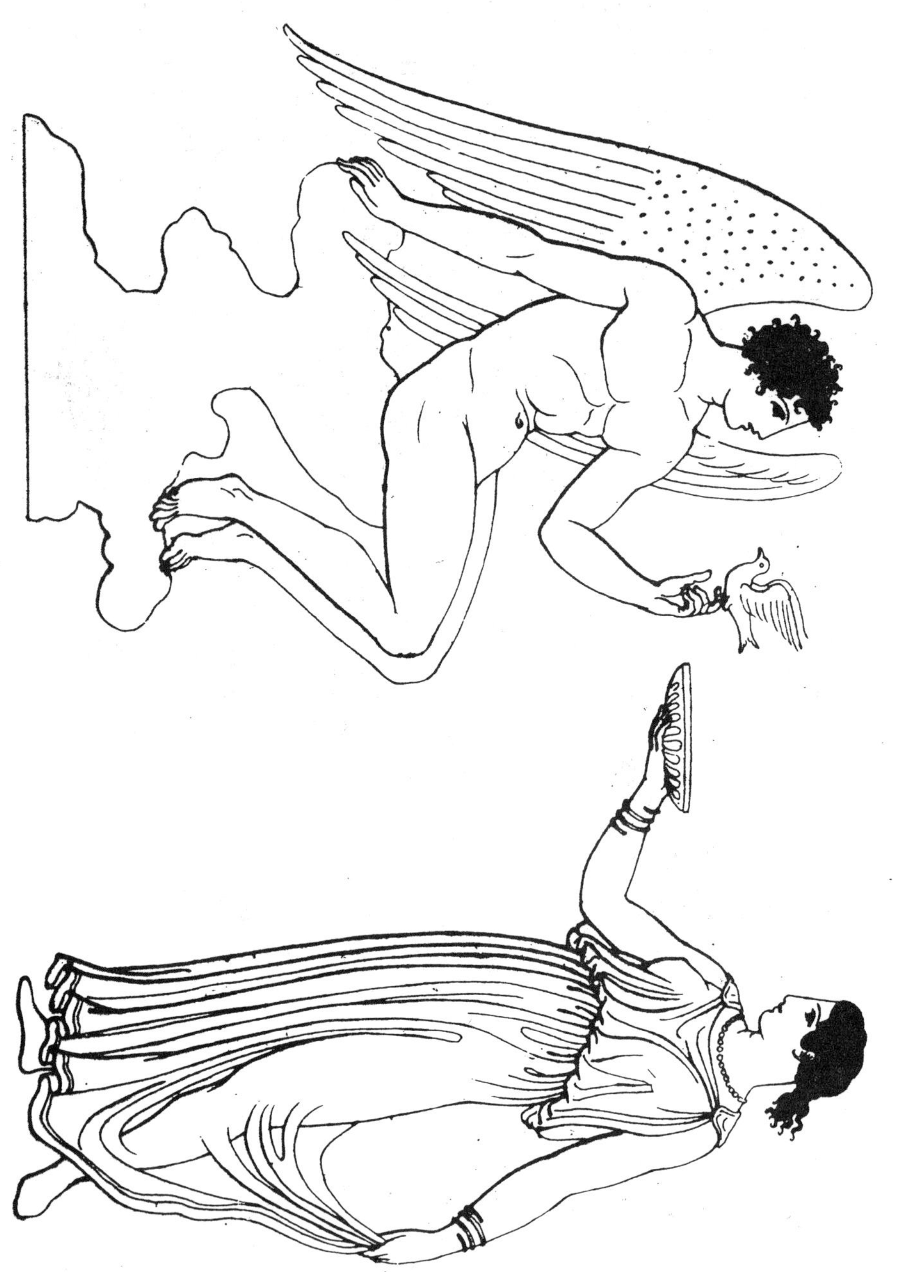

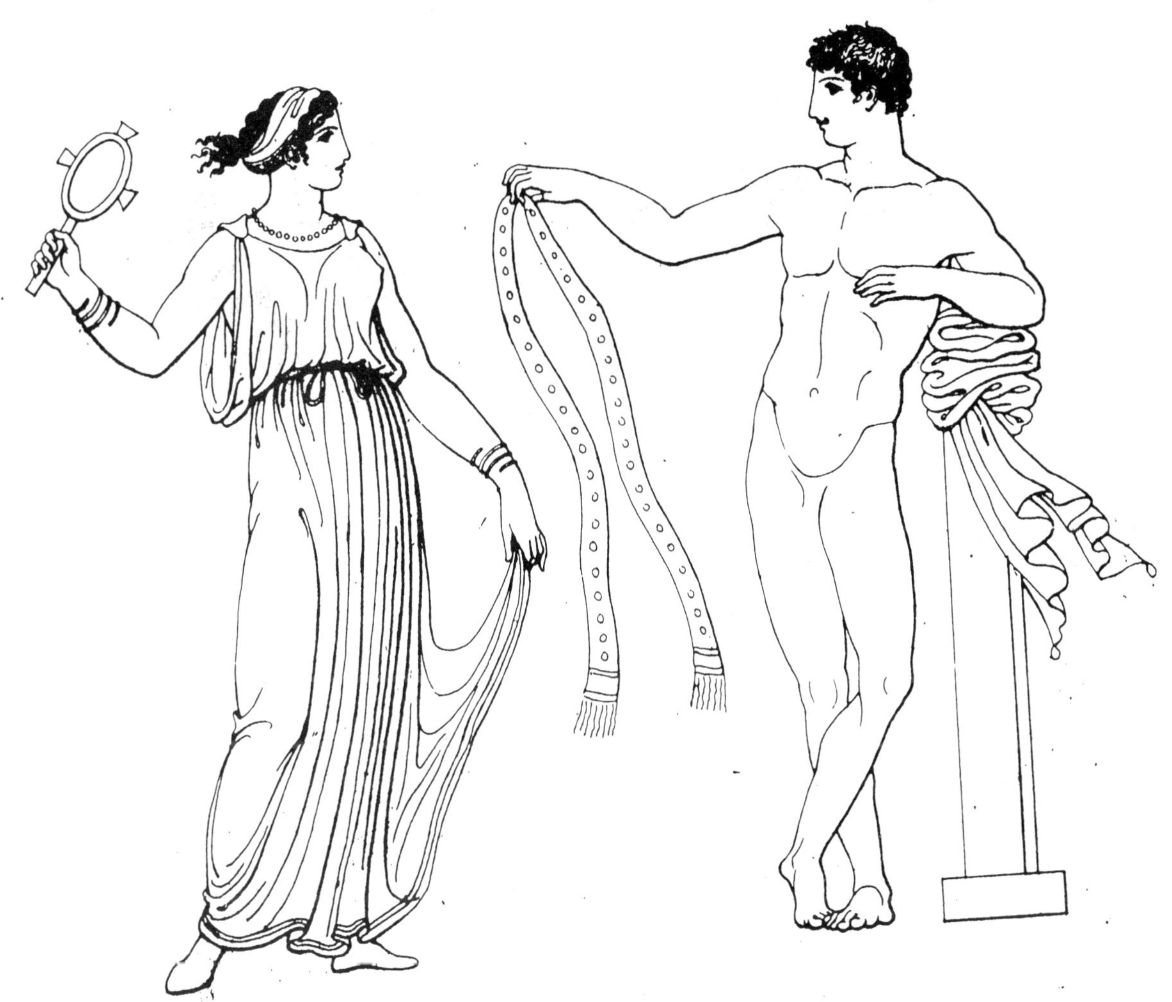

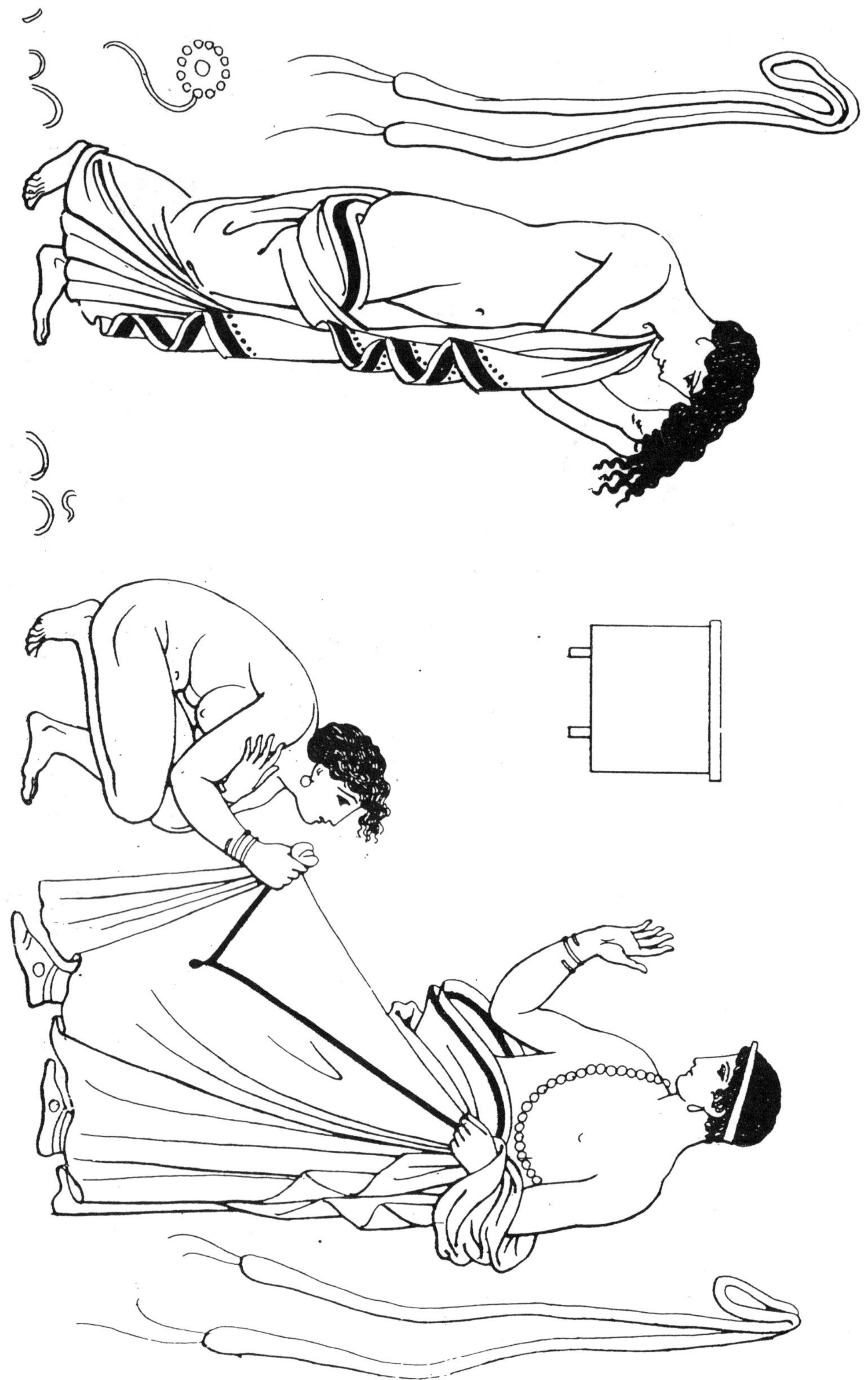

27:28(b)

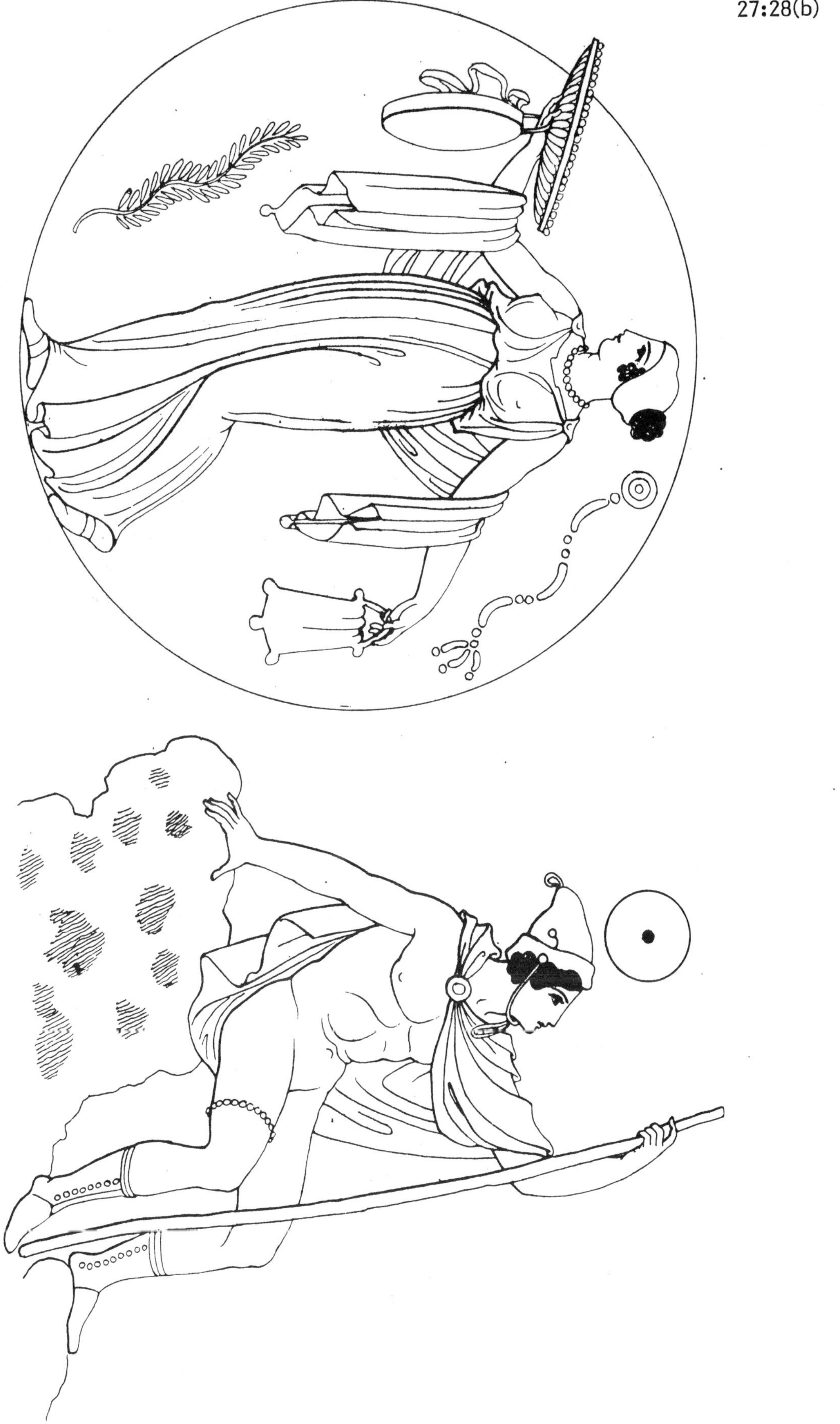

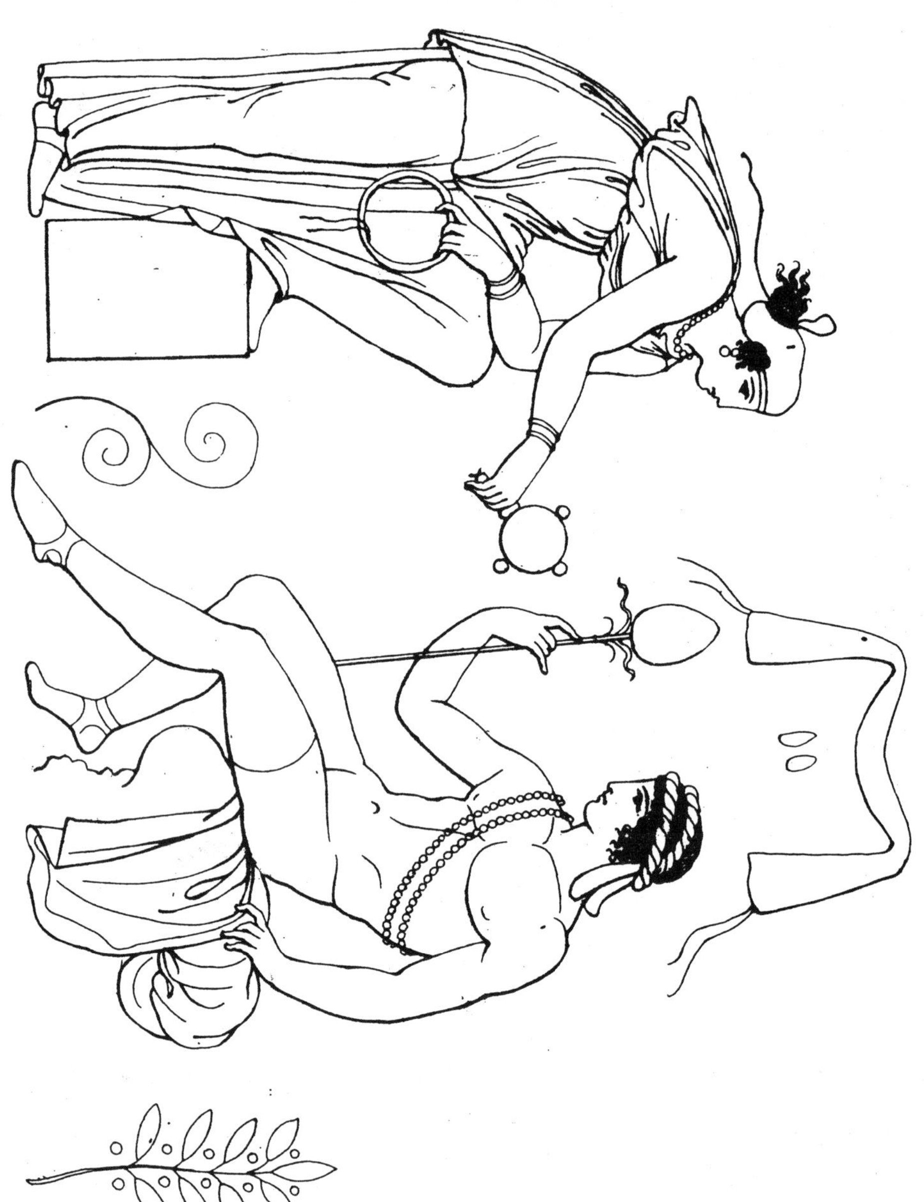

29:30

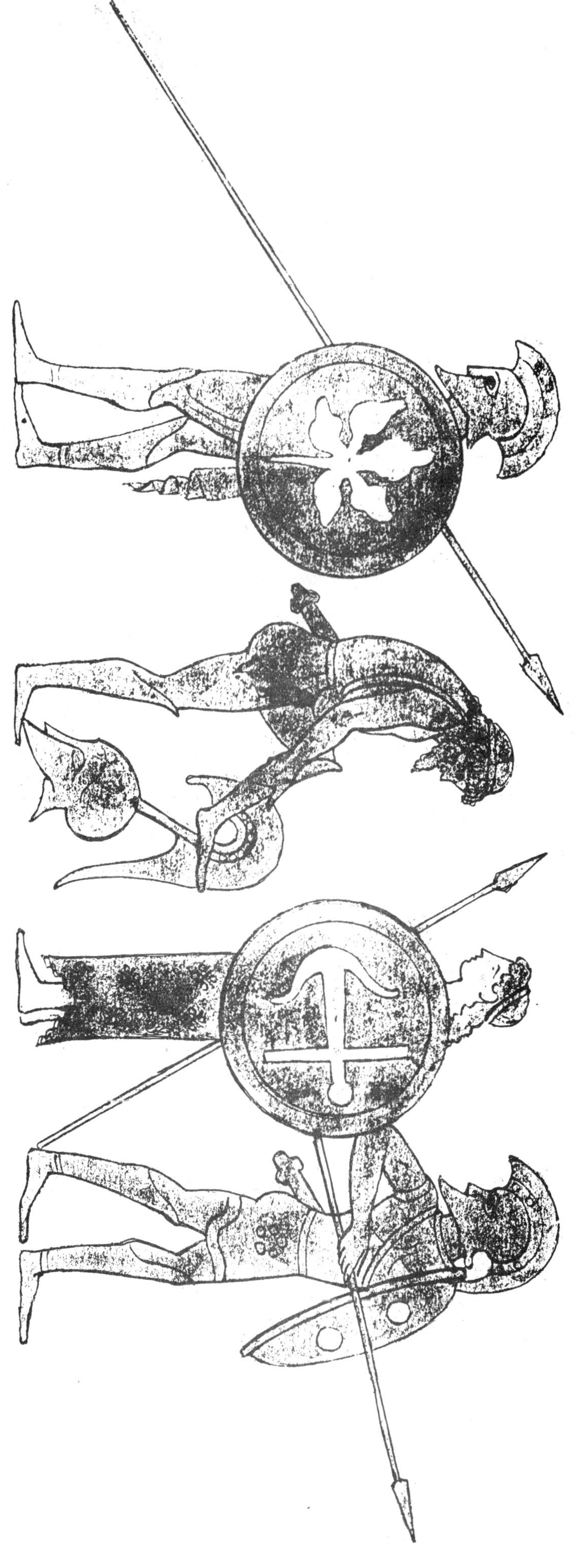

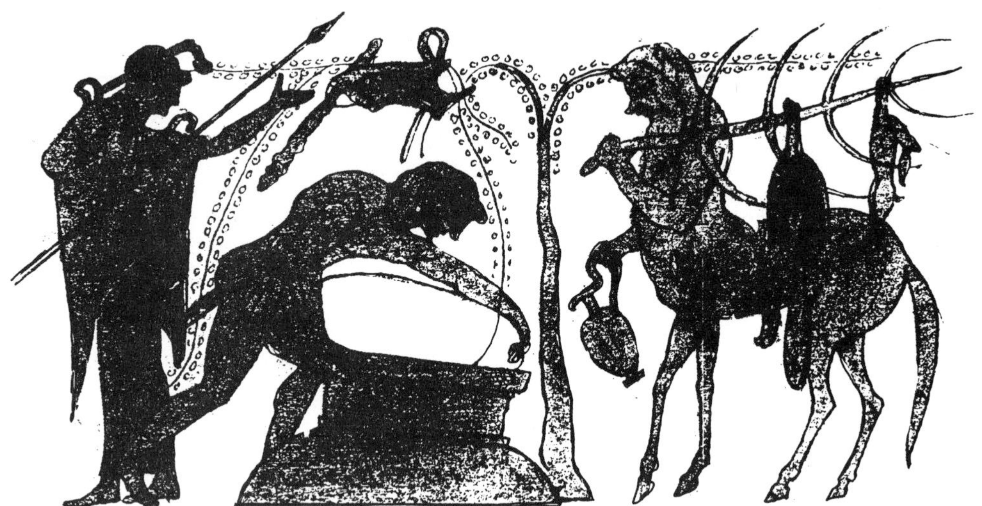

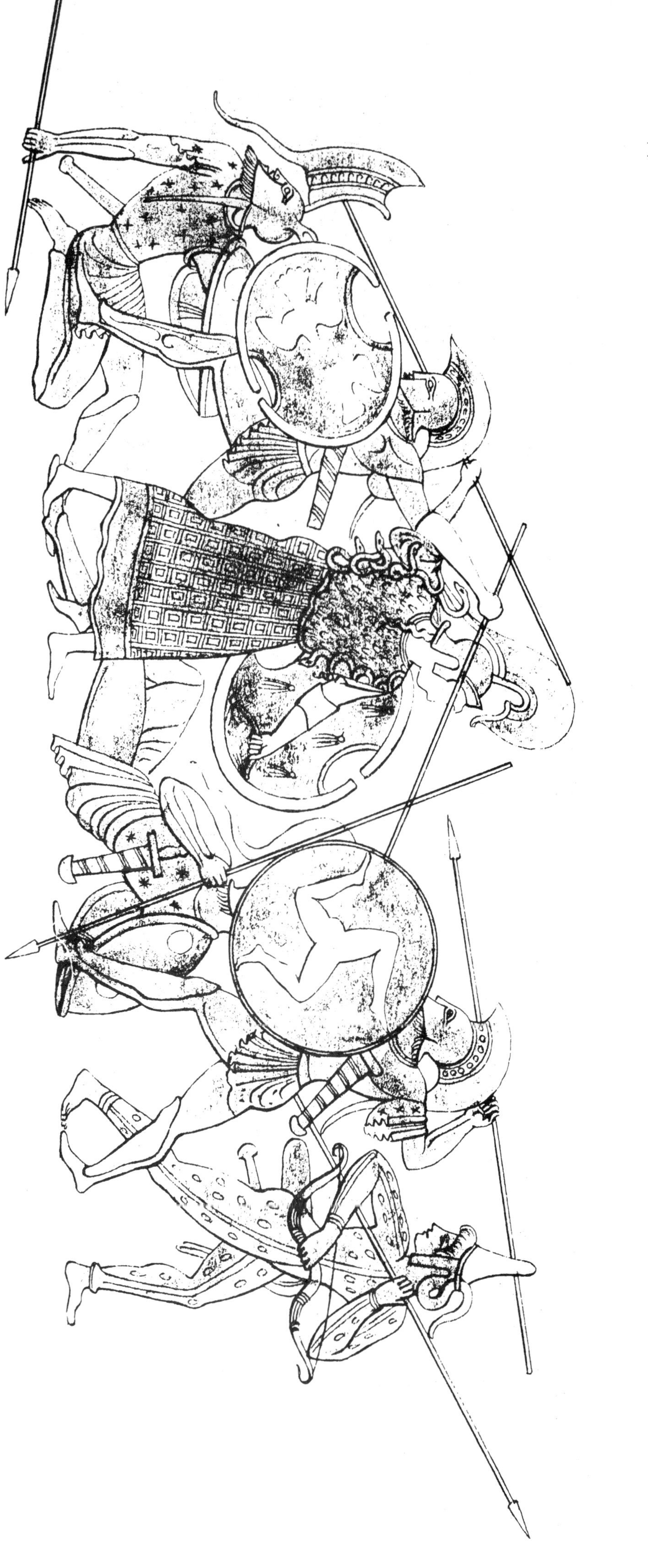

30:32

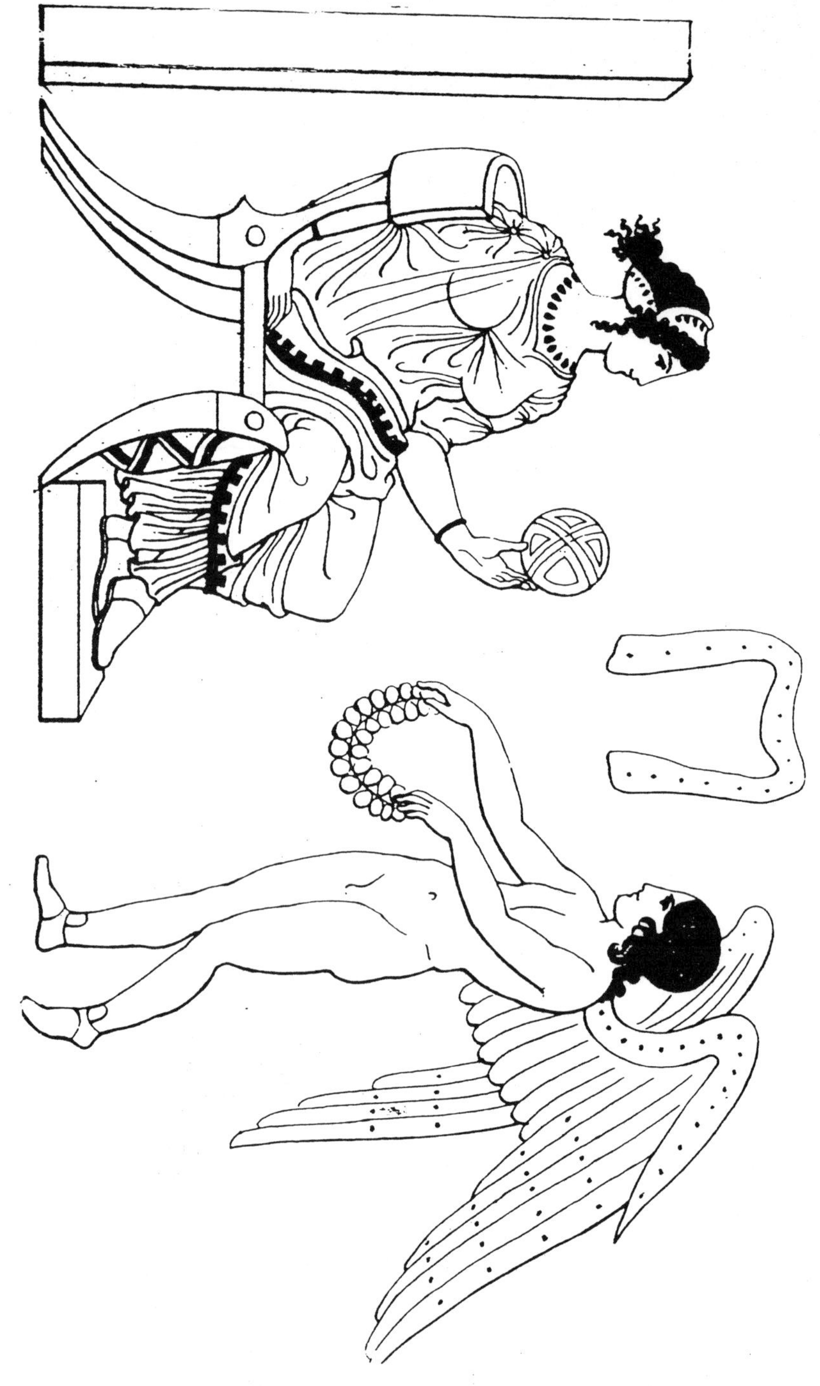

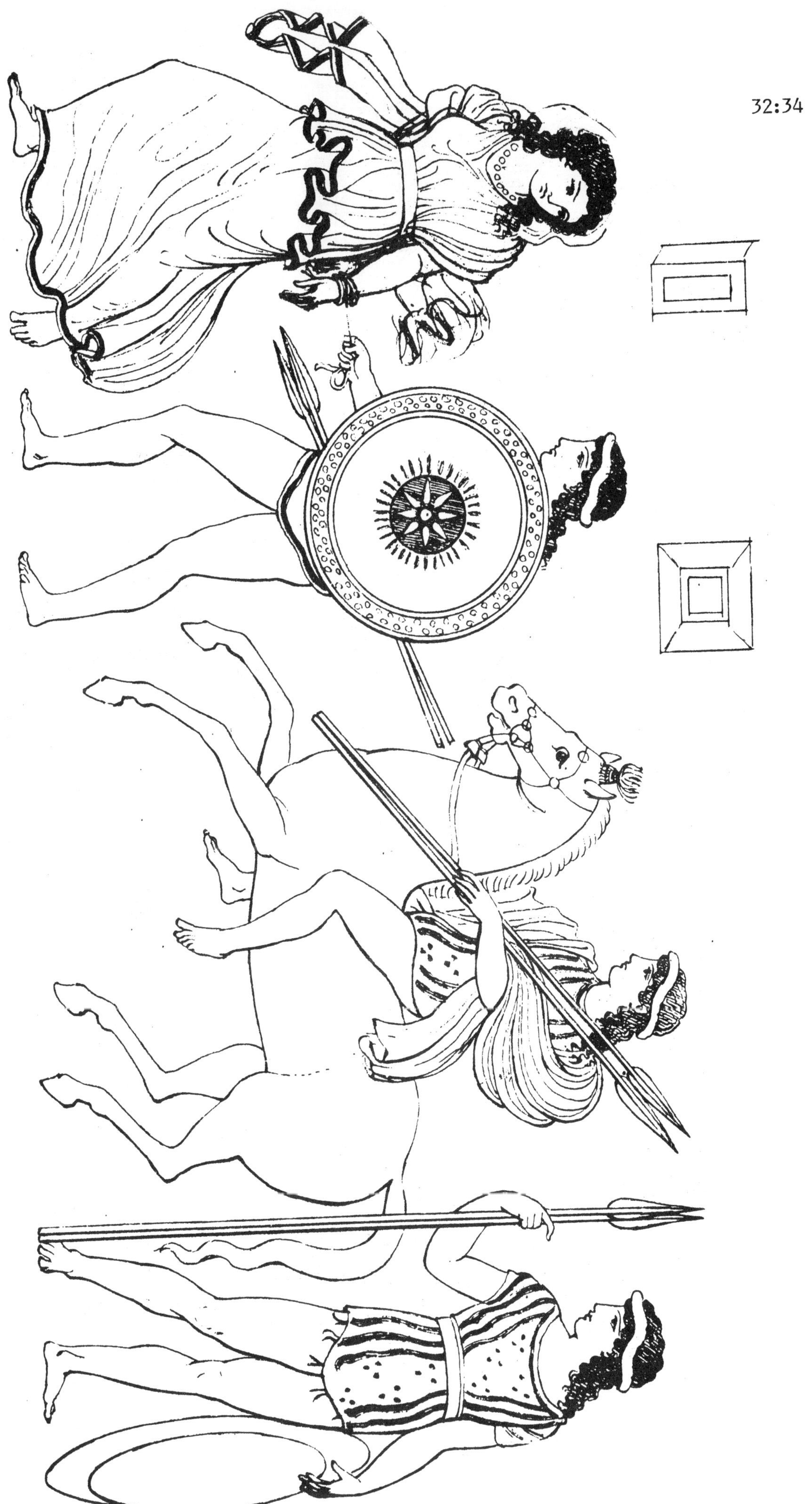

32:34

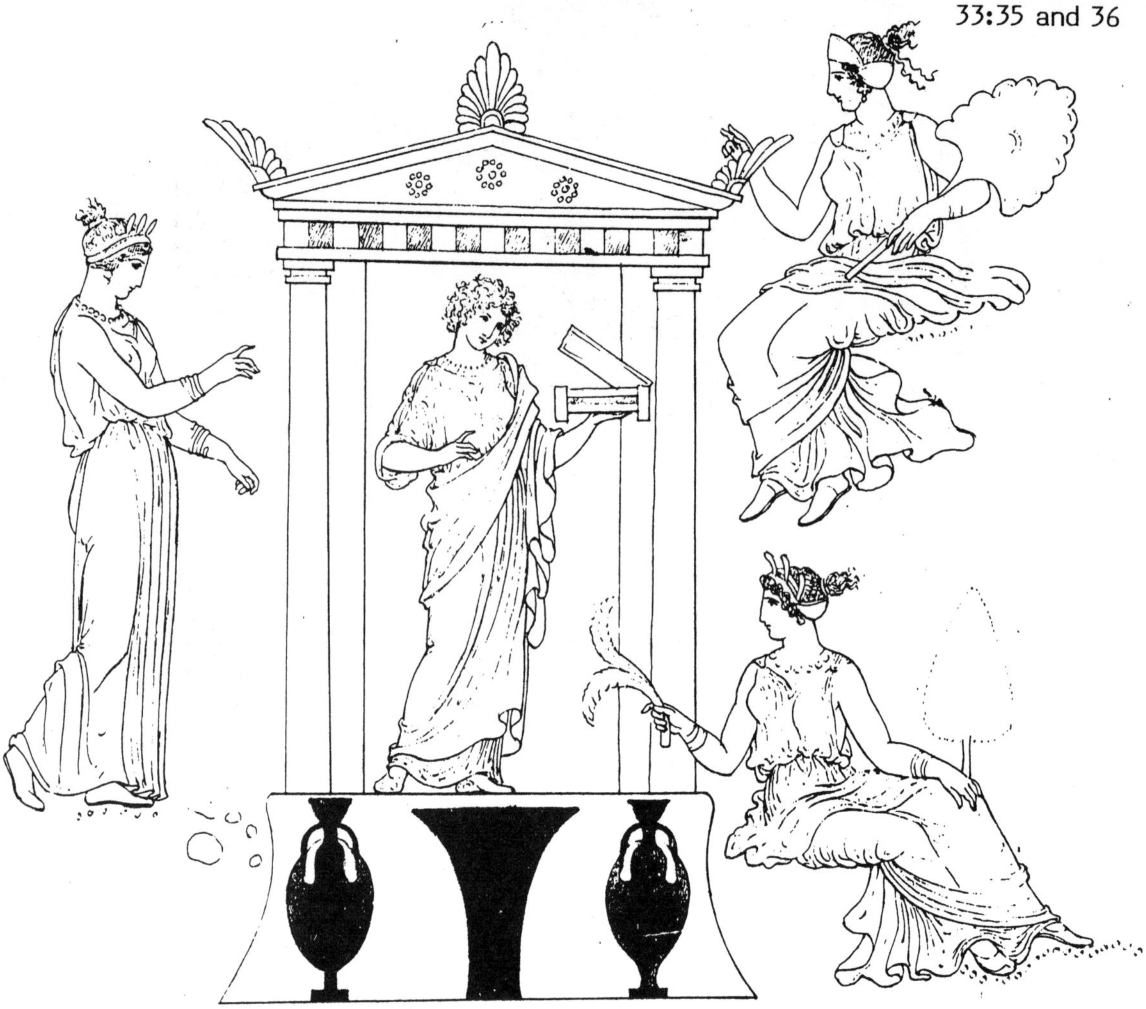

33:35 and 36

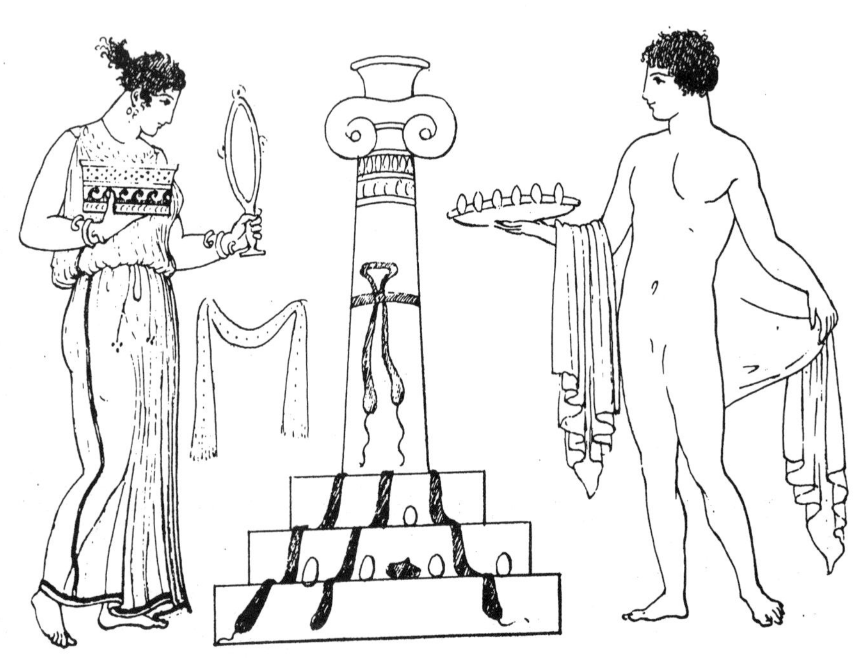

34:37(i) and (ii)

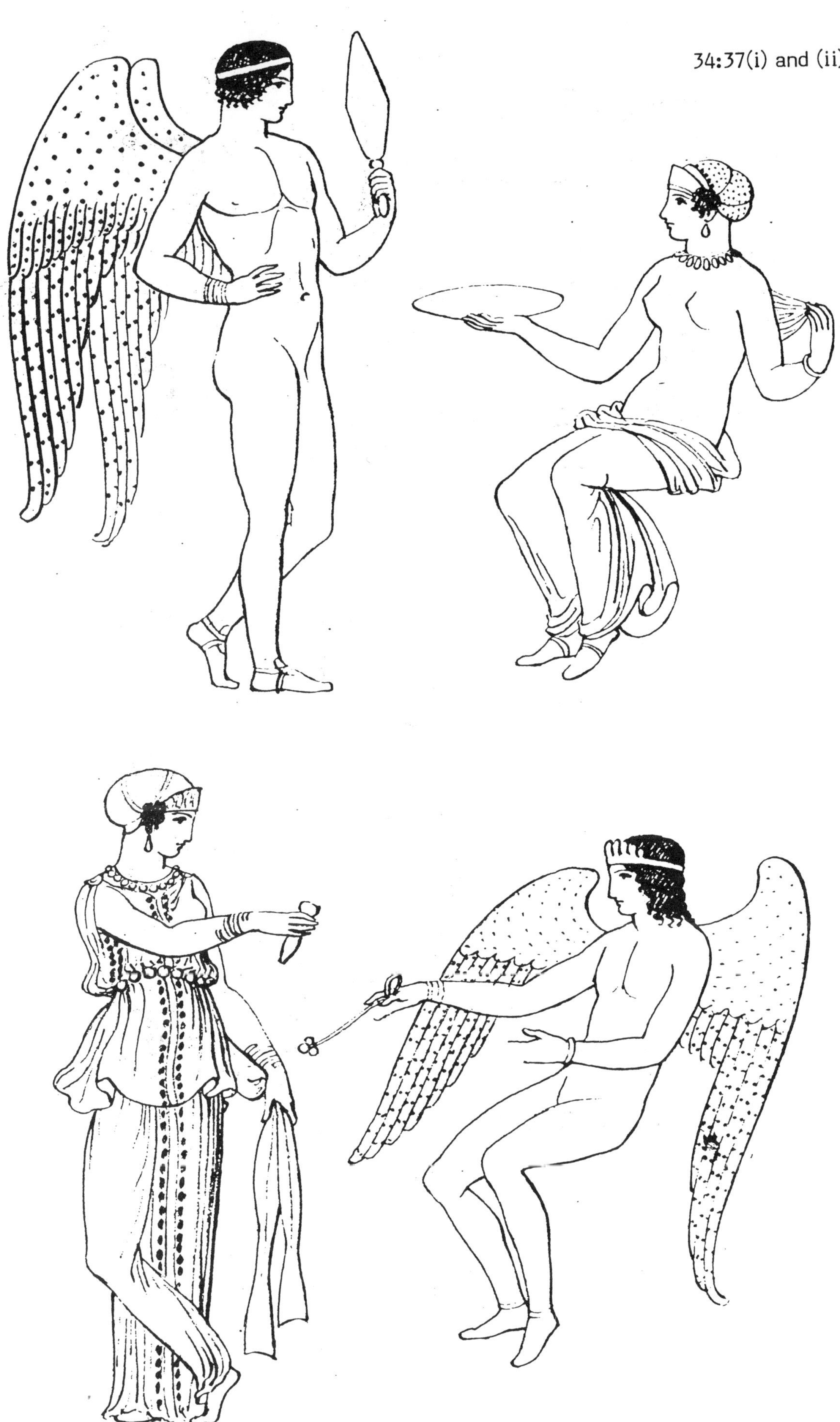

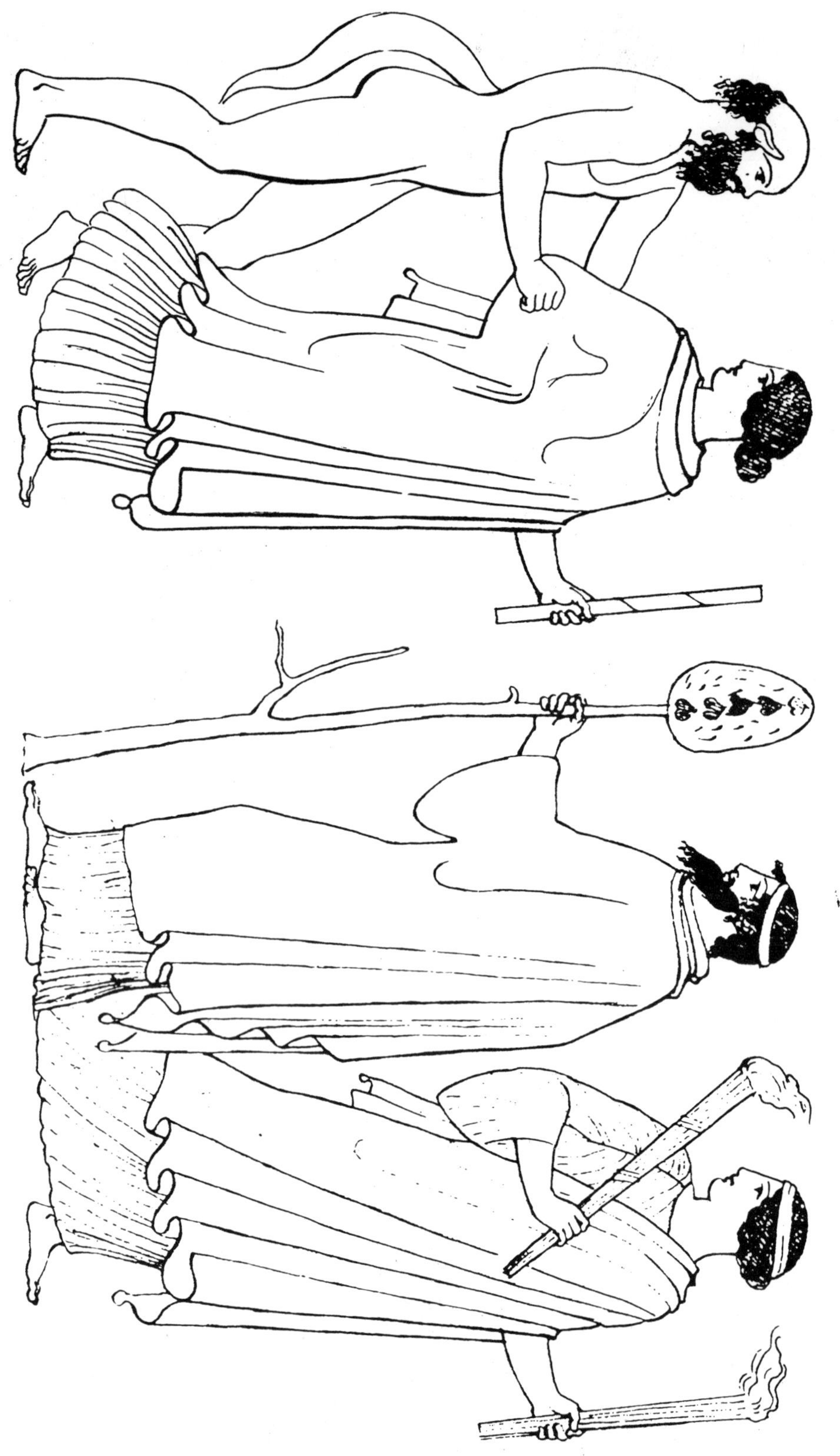

43:47

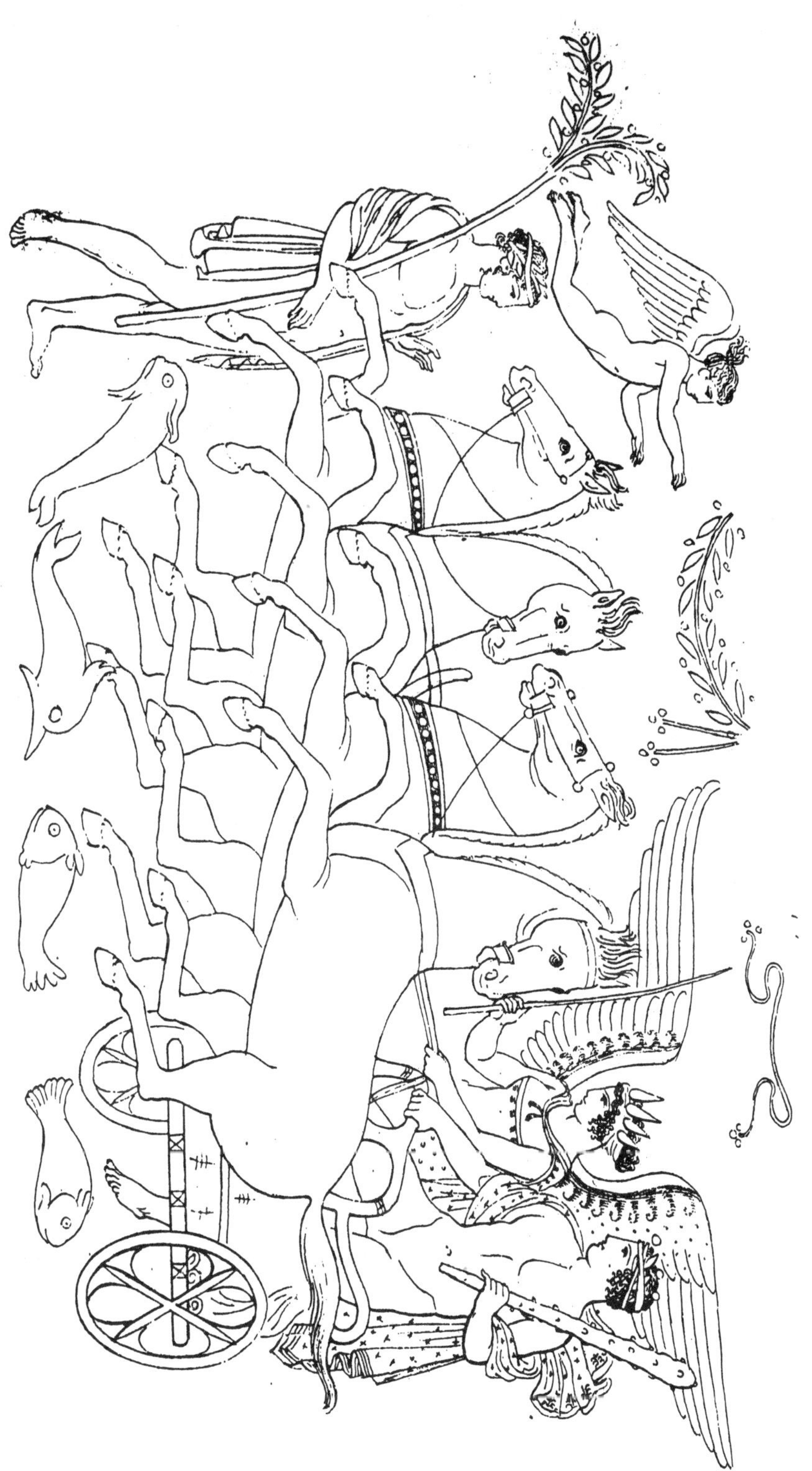

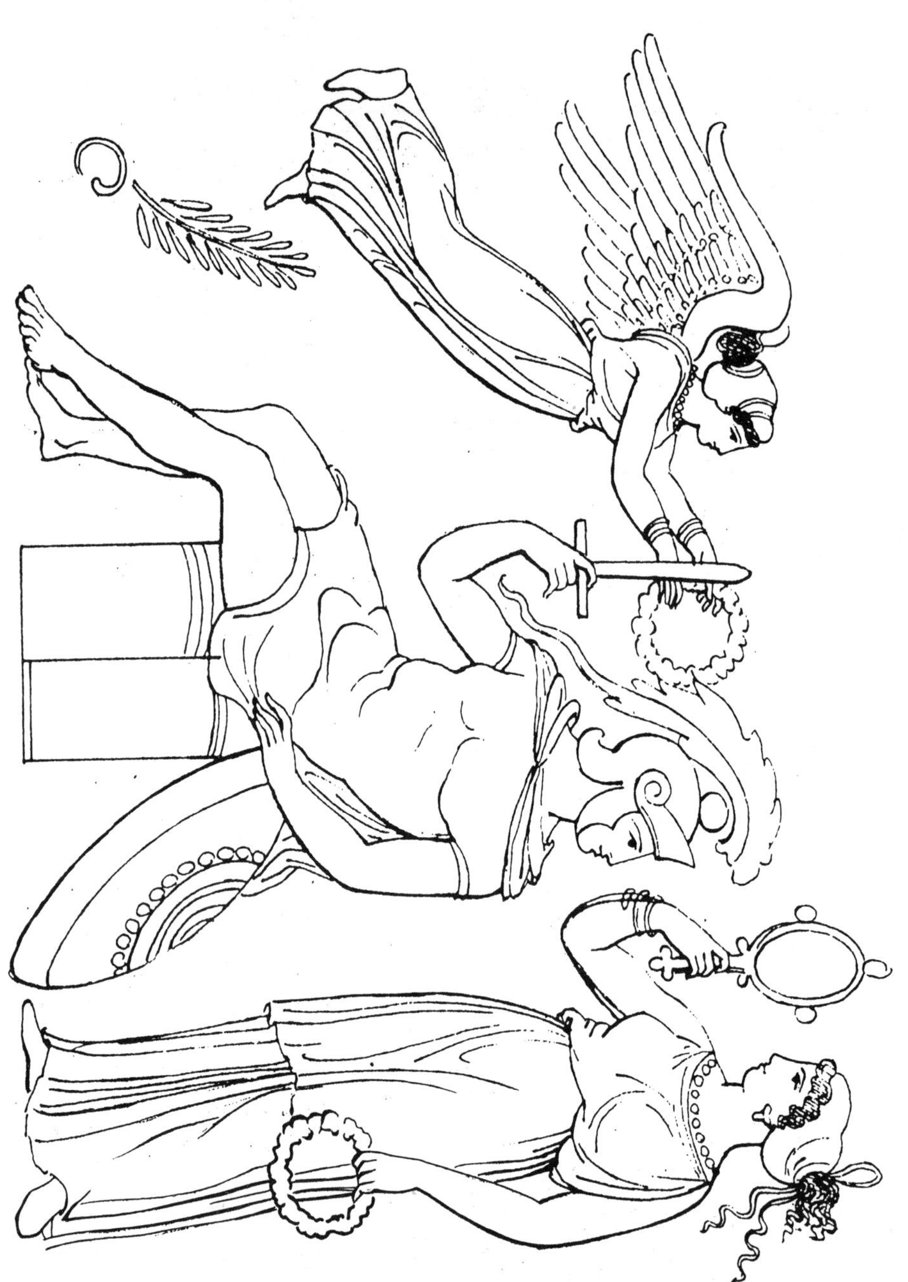

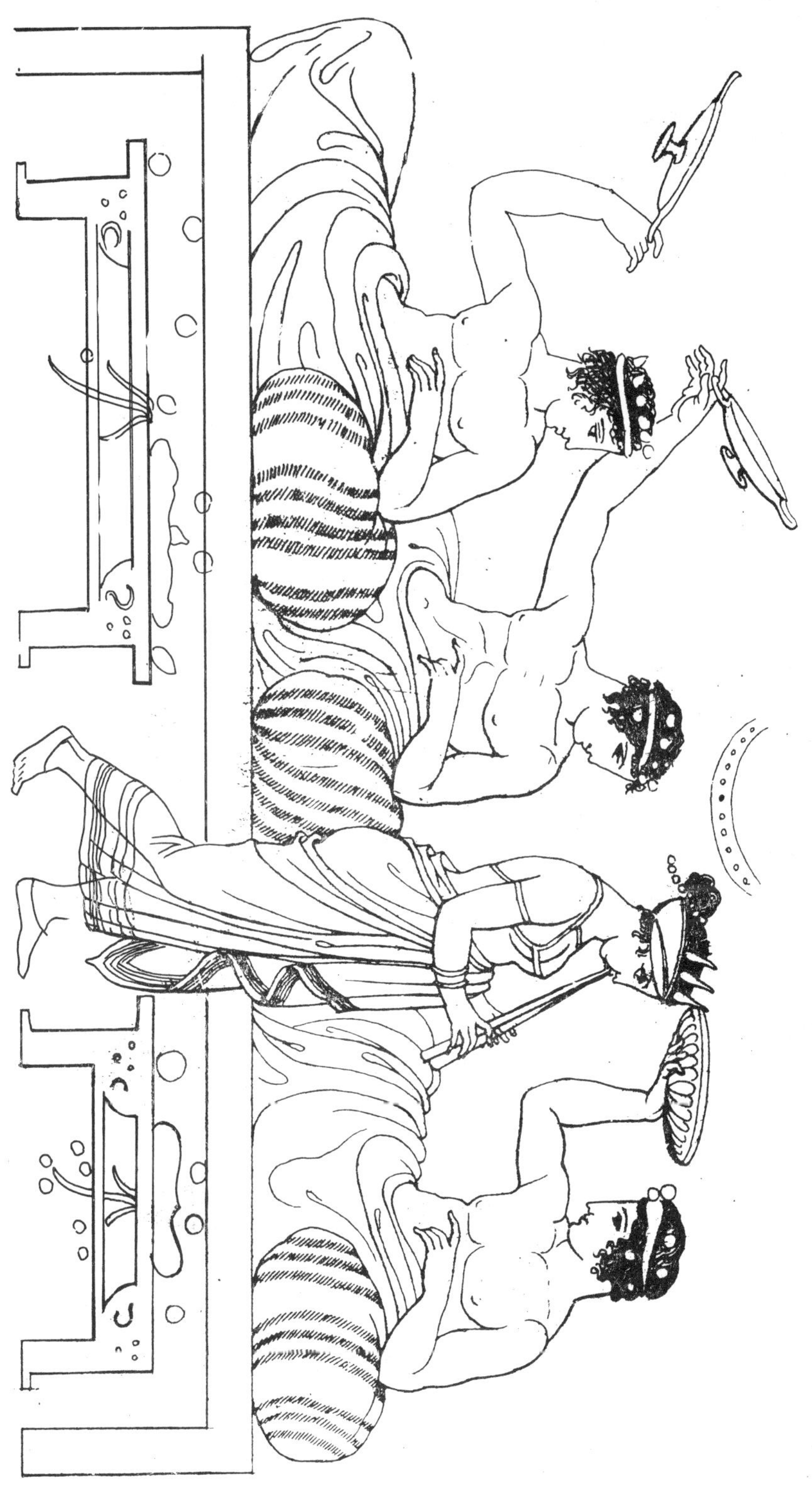

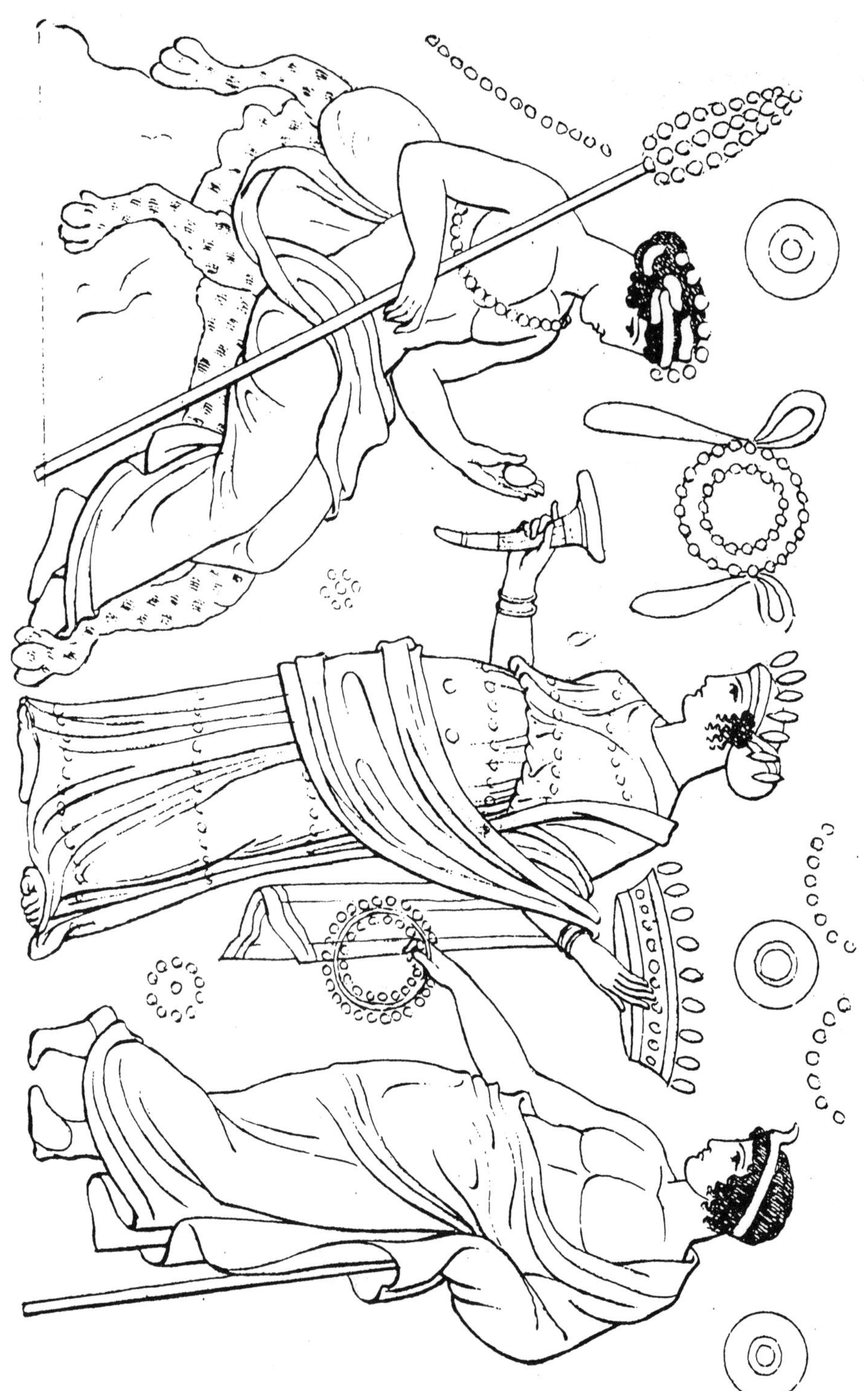

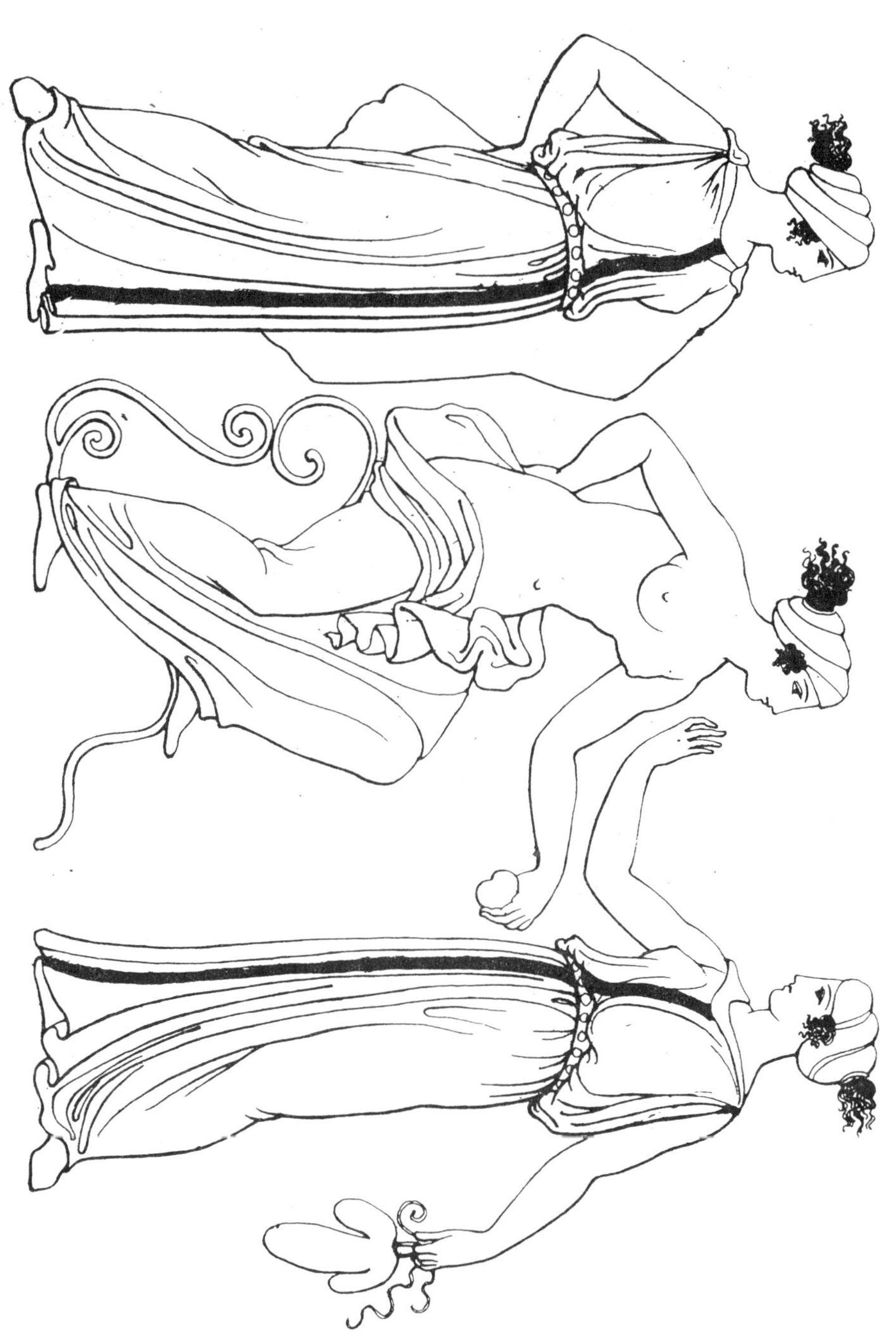

48:52(b)

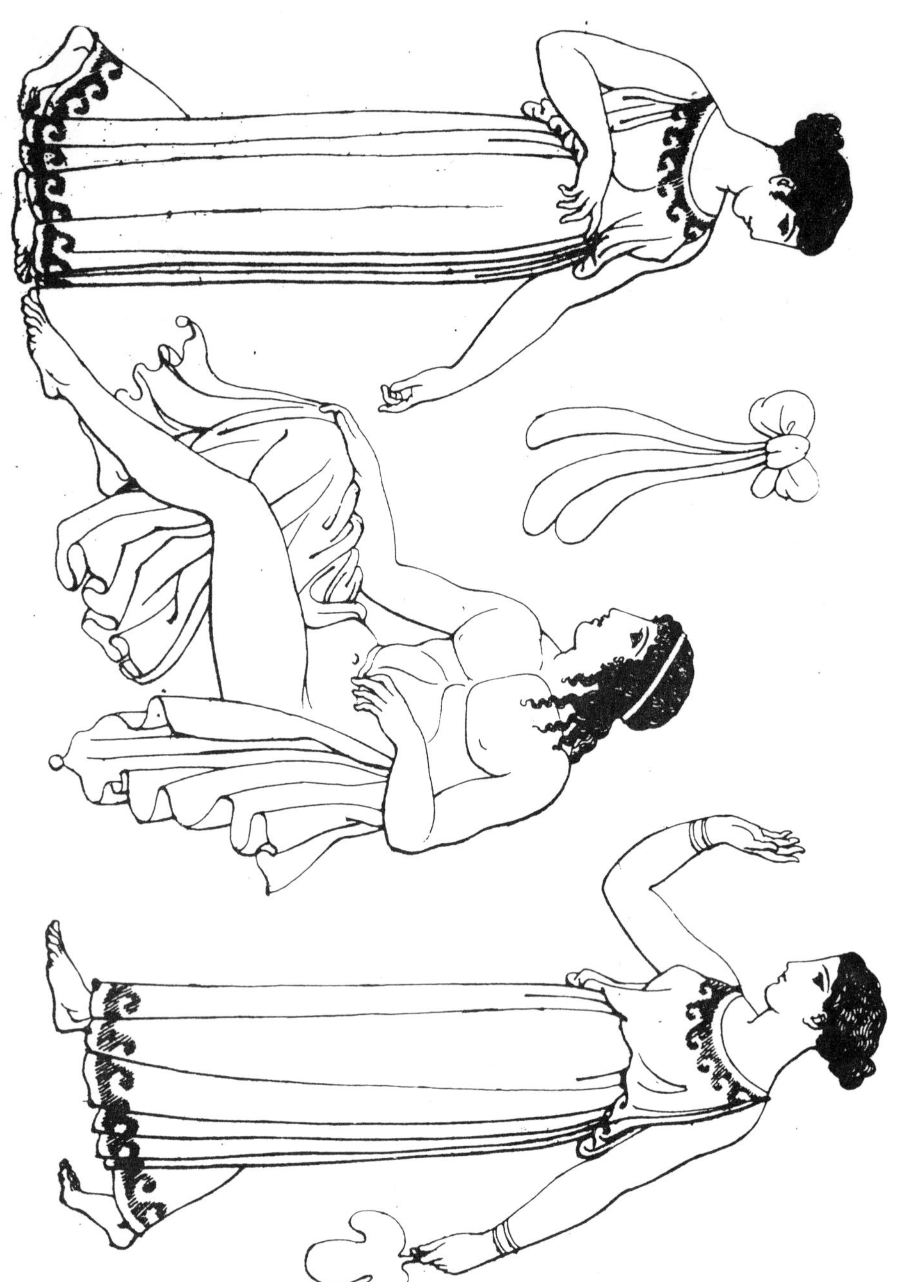

50:54(b)

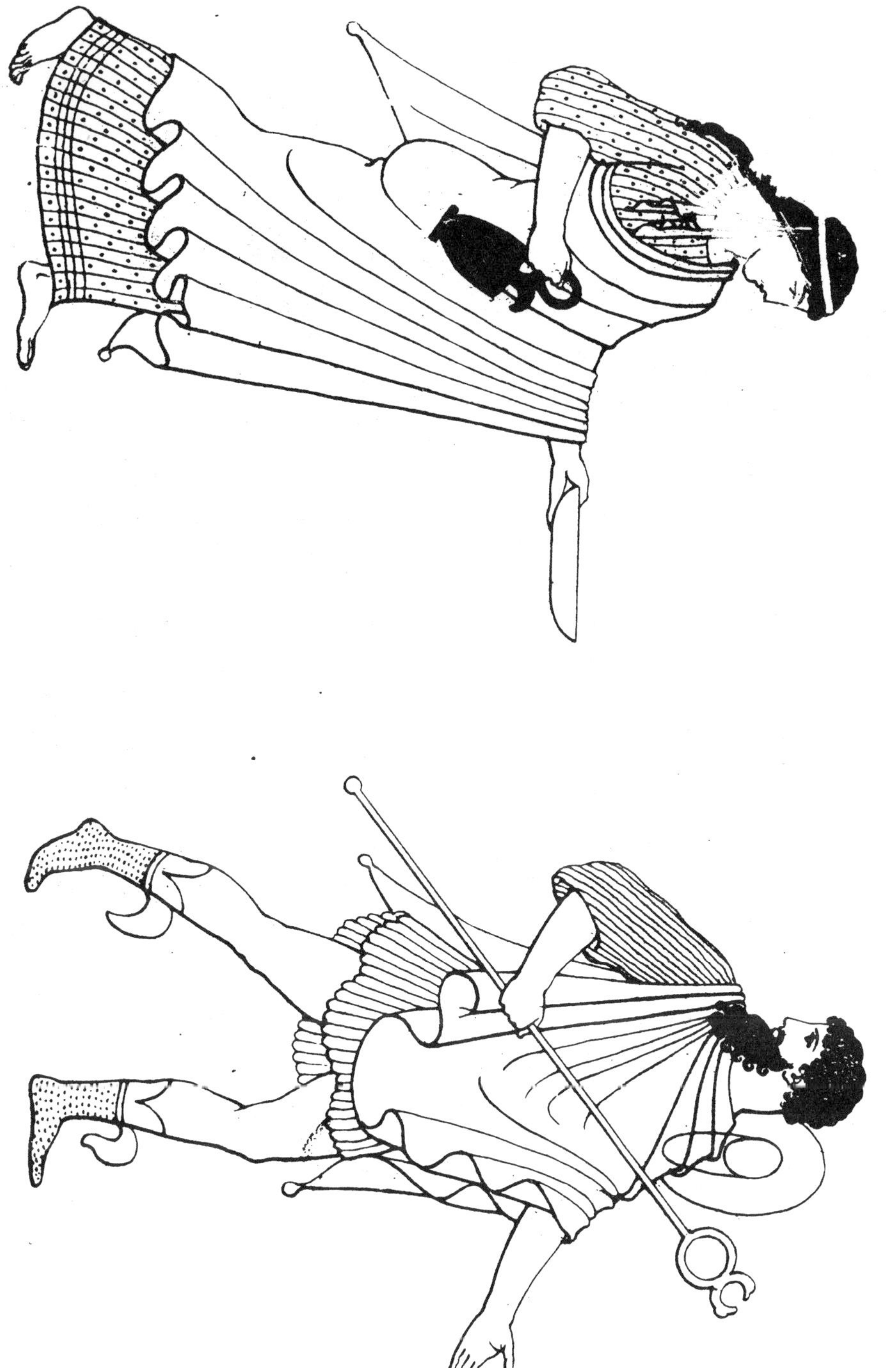

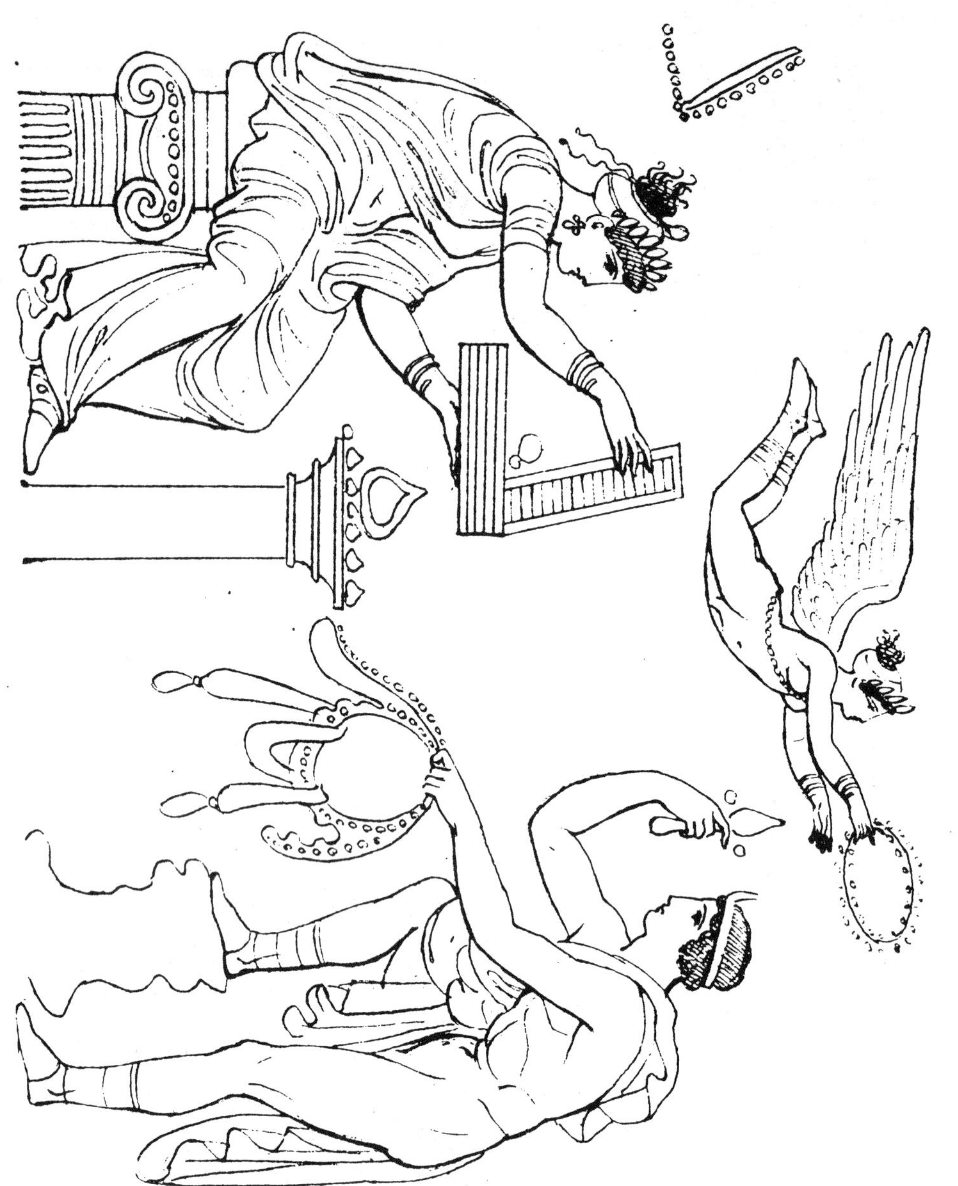

51:56

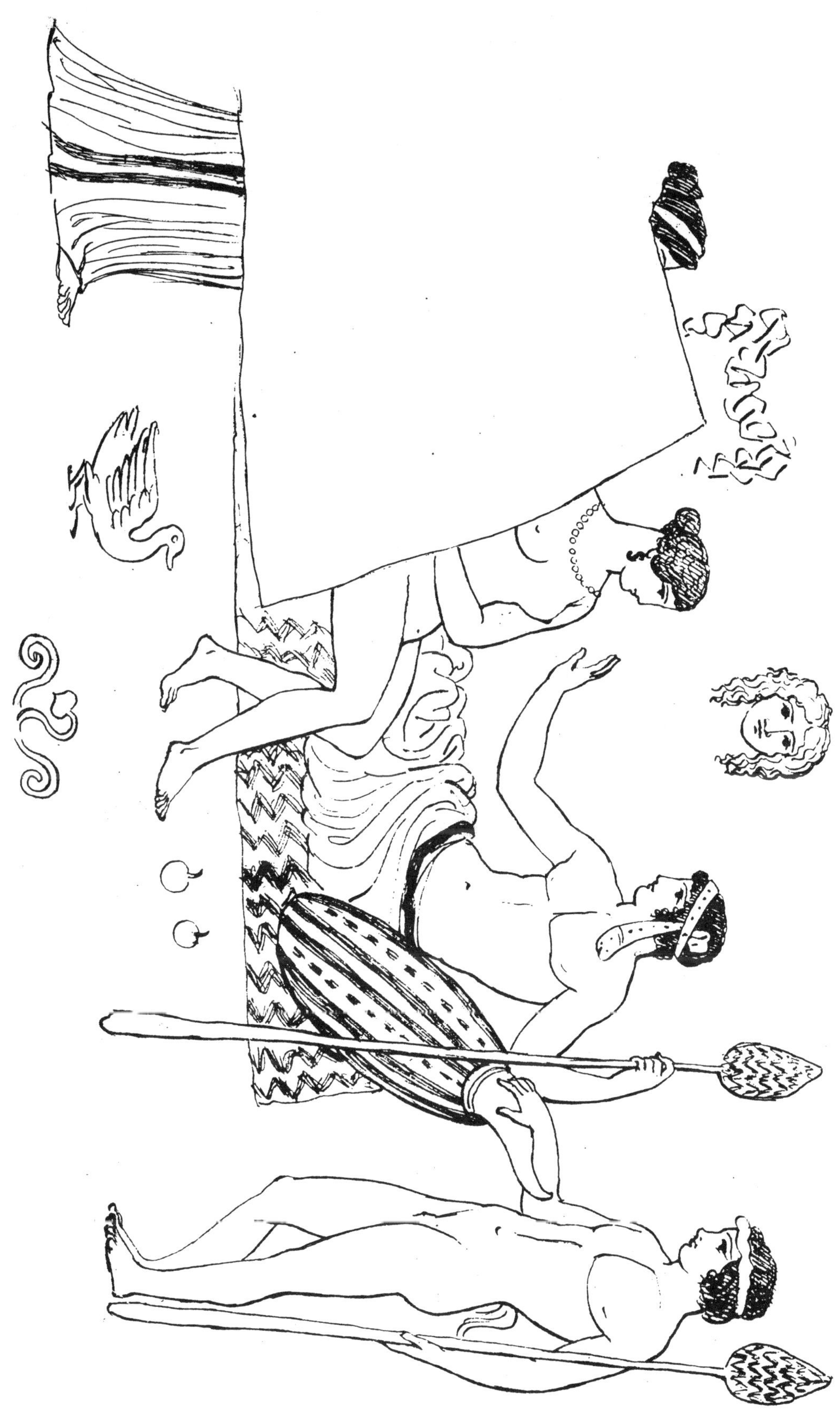

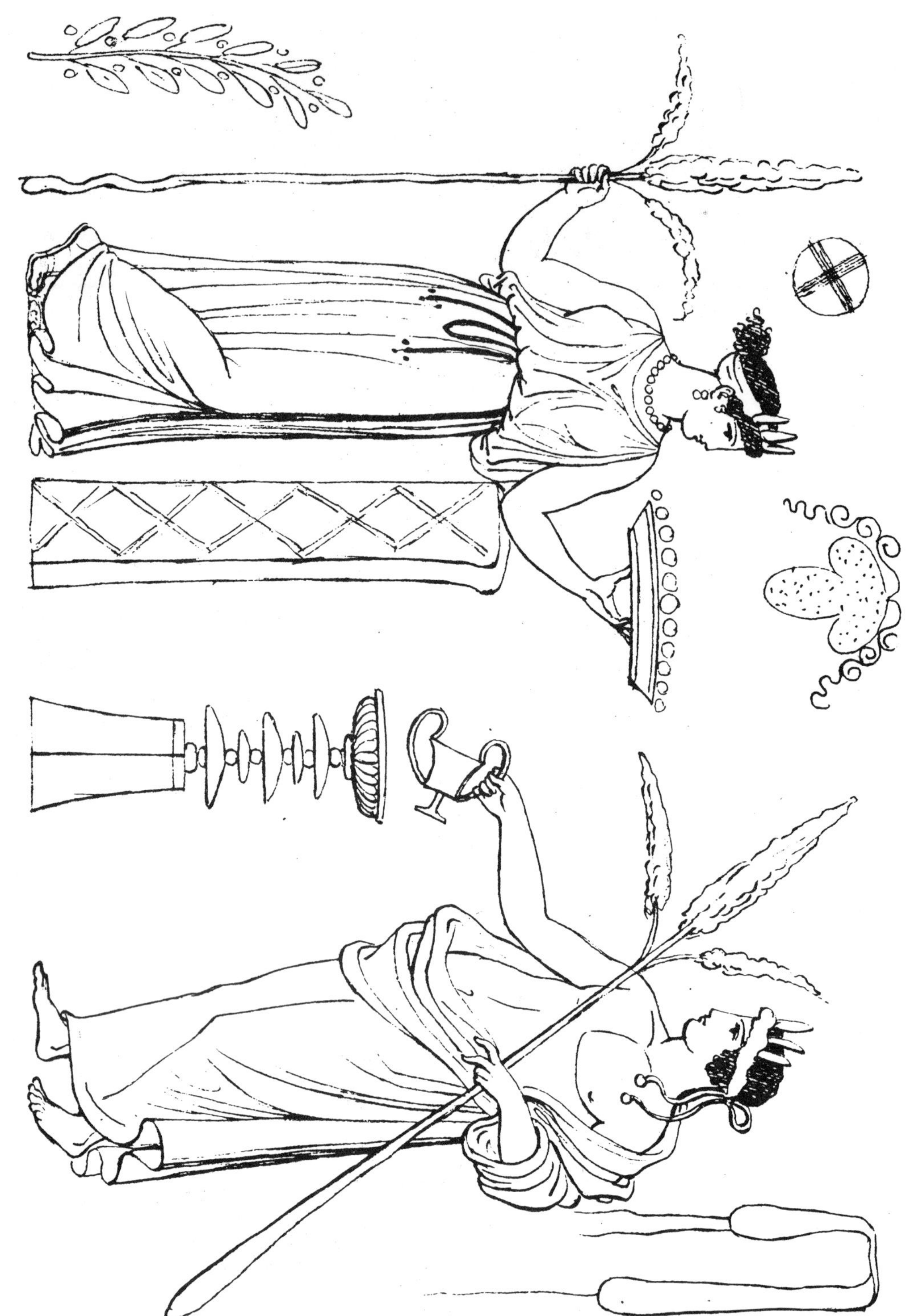

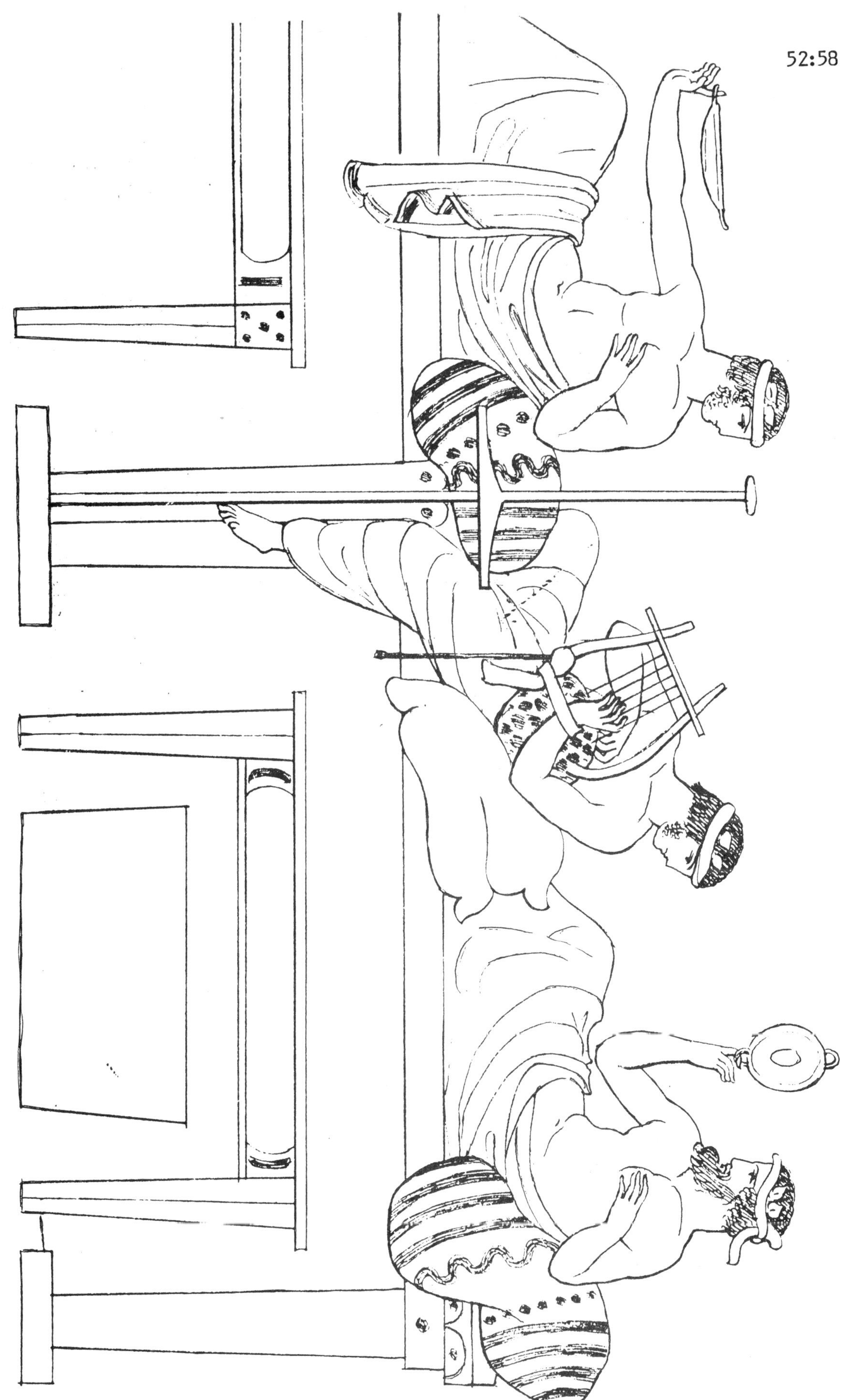

52:58

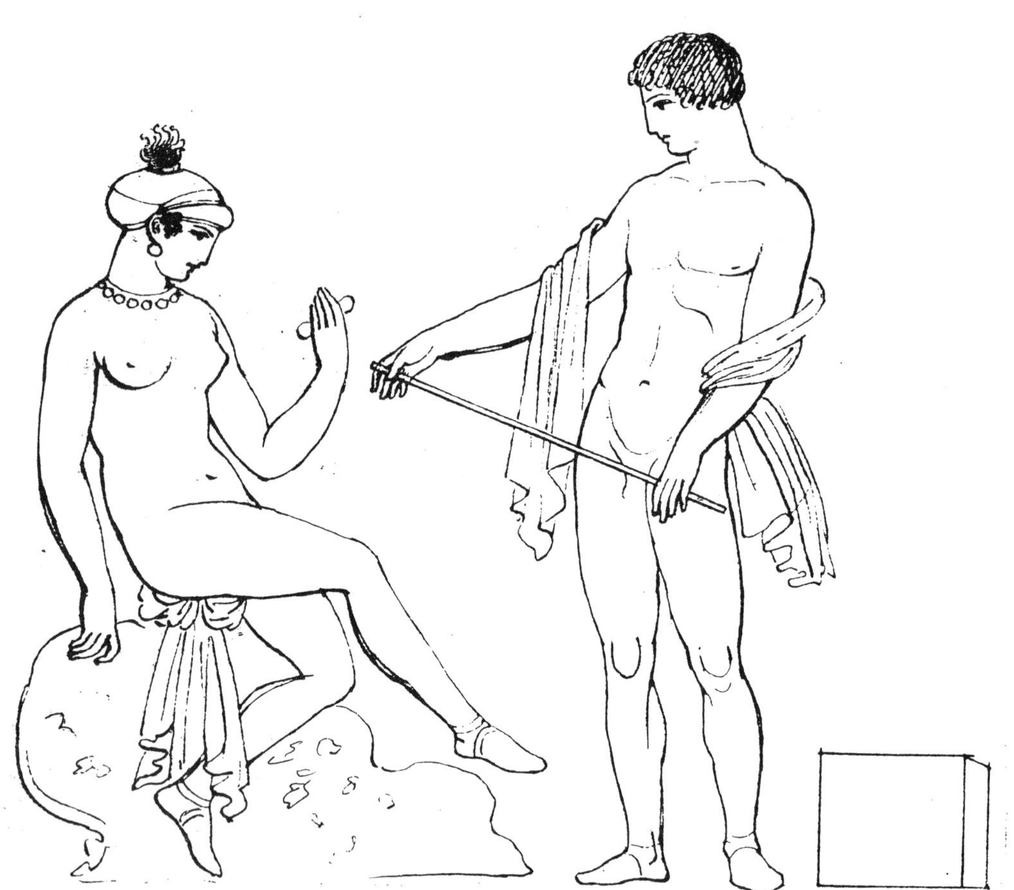

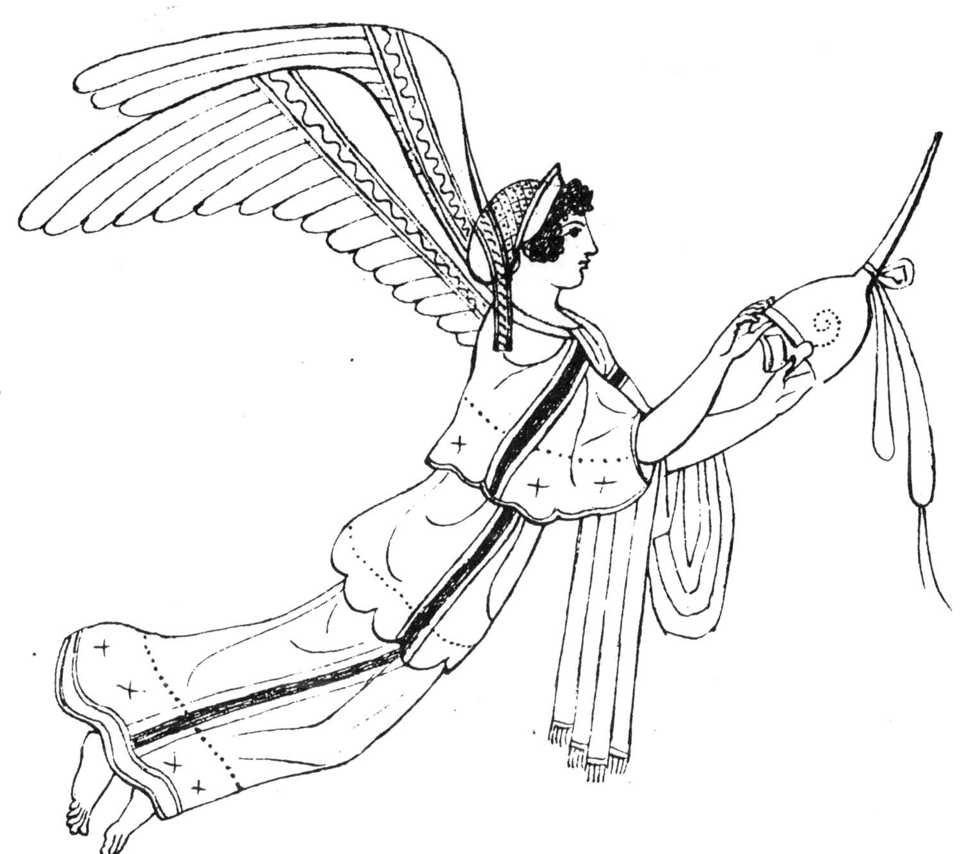

55:61(i), (ii) and (iii)

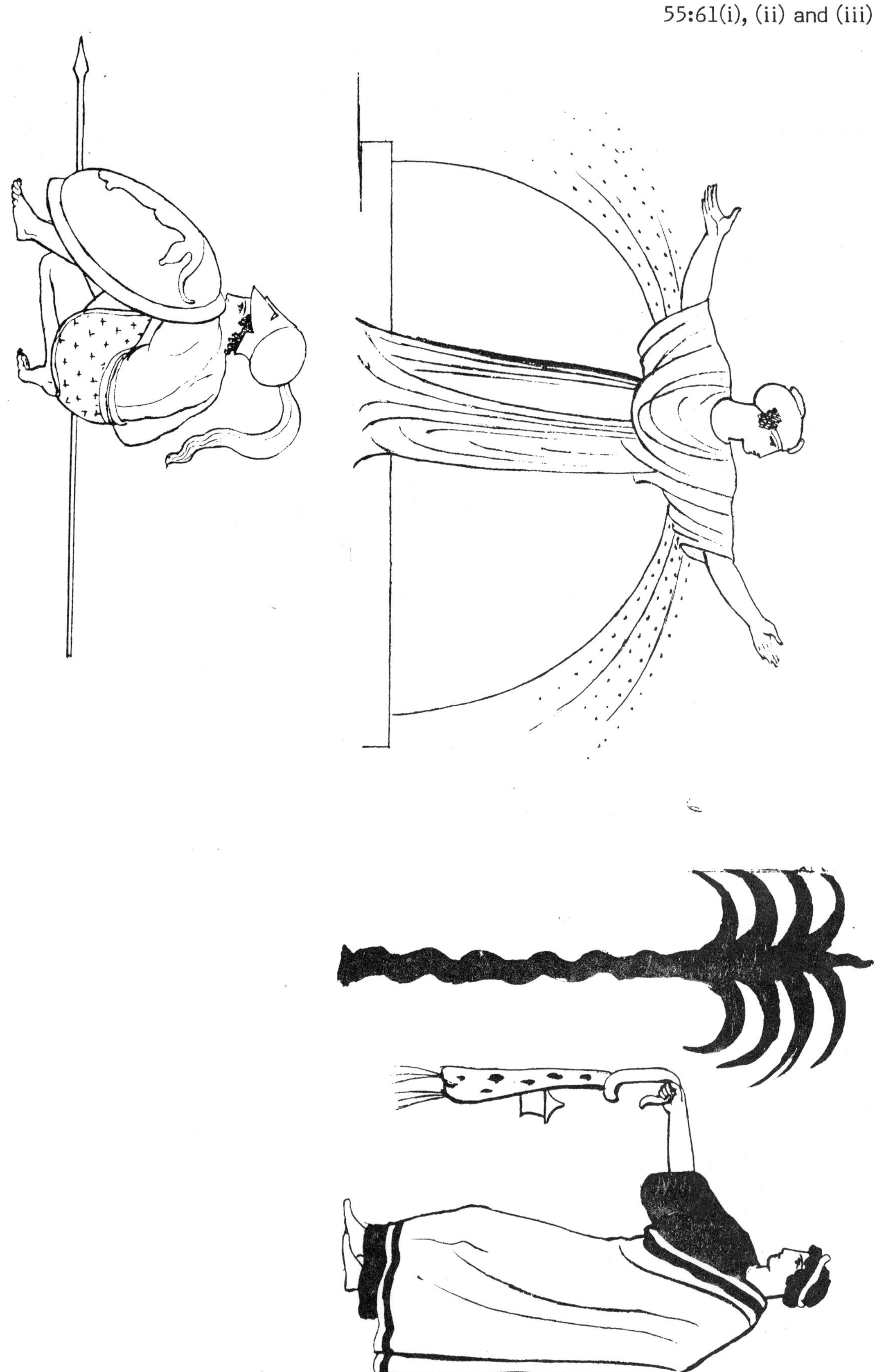

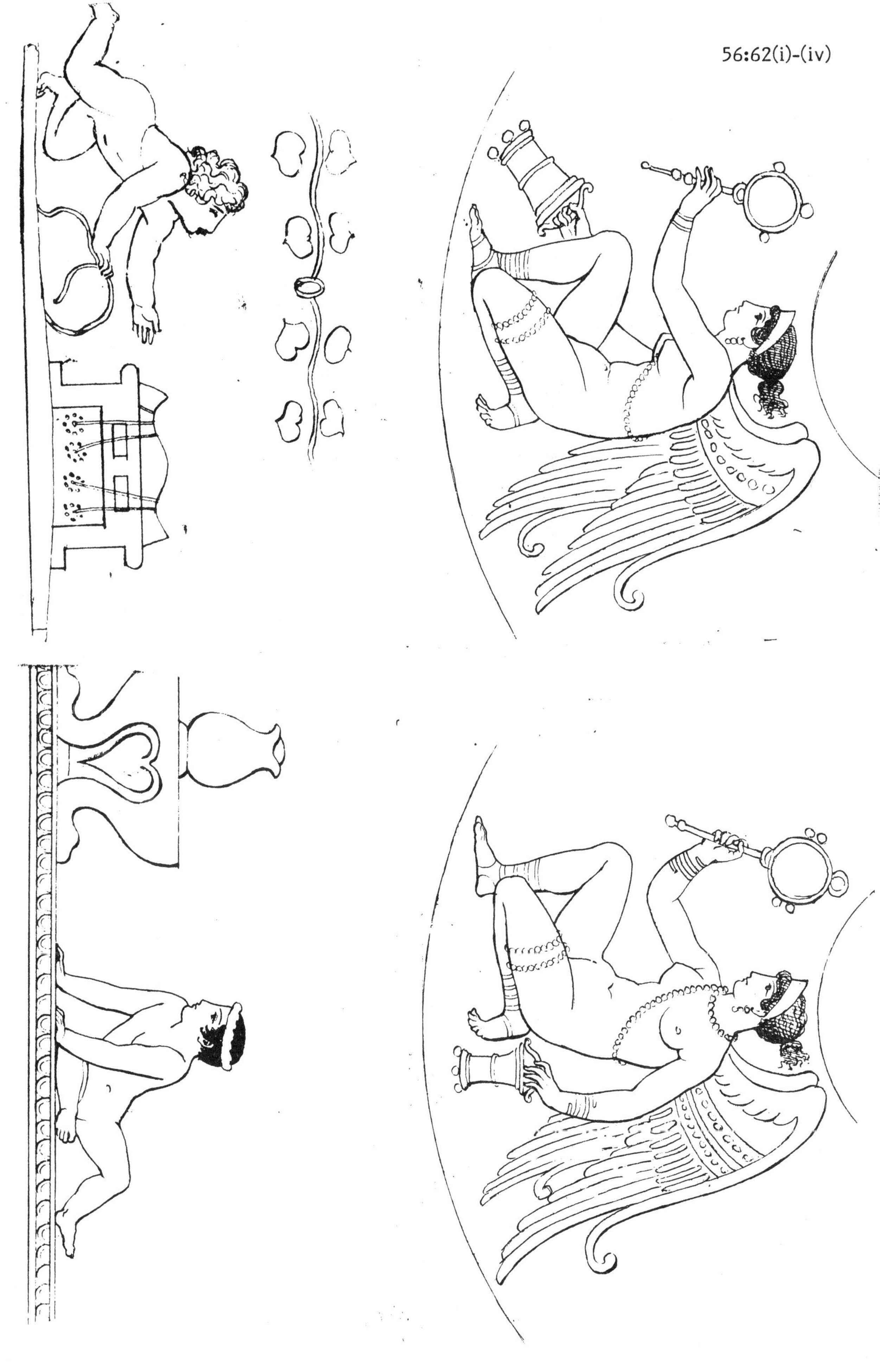

56:62(i)-(iv)

57:63(i)

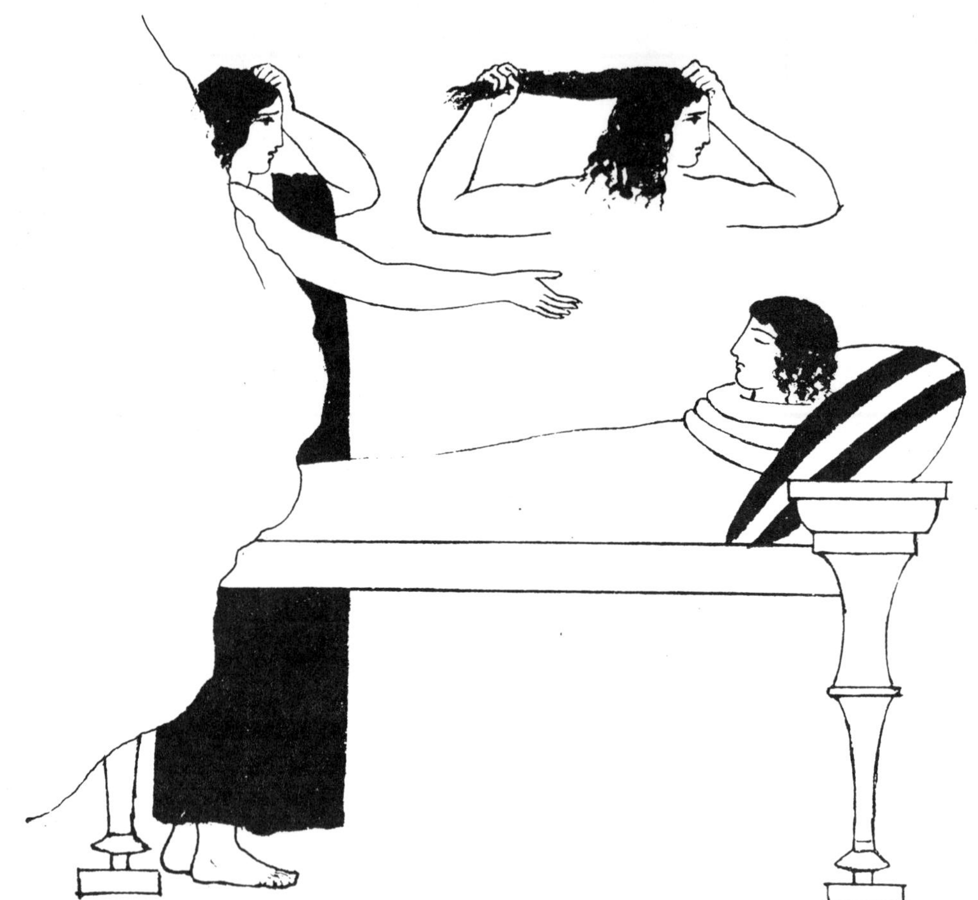

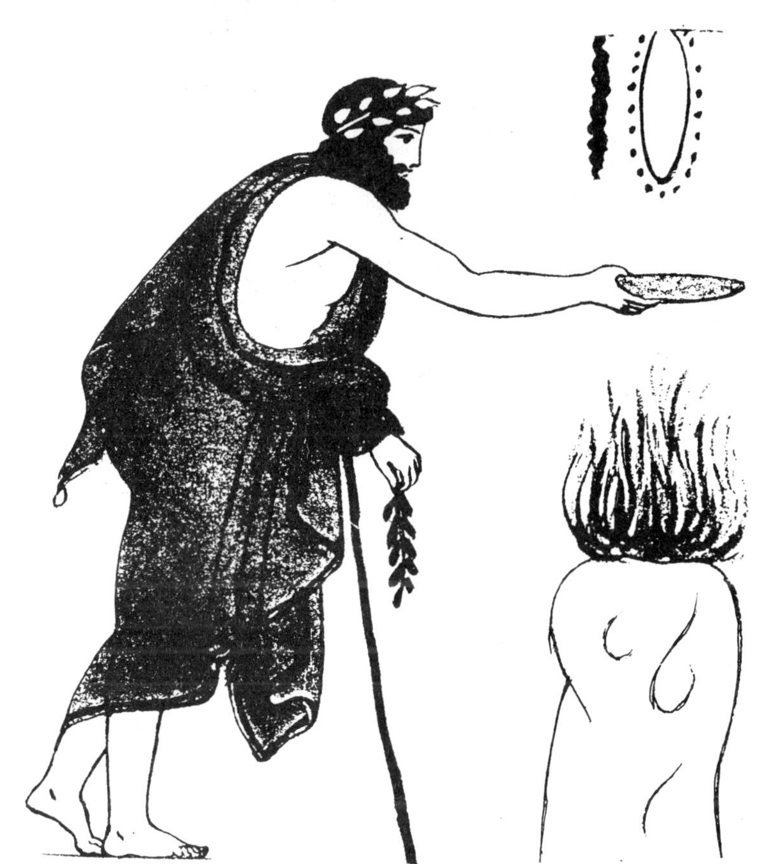

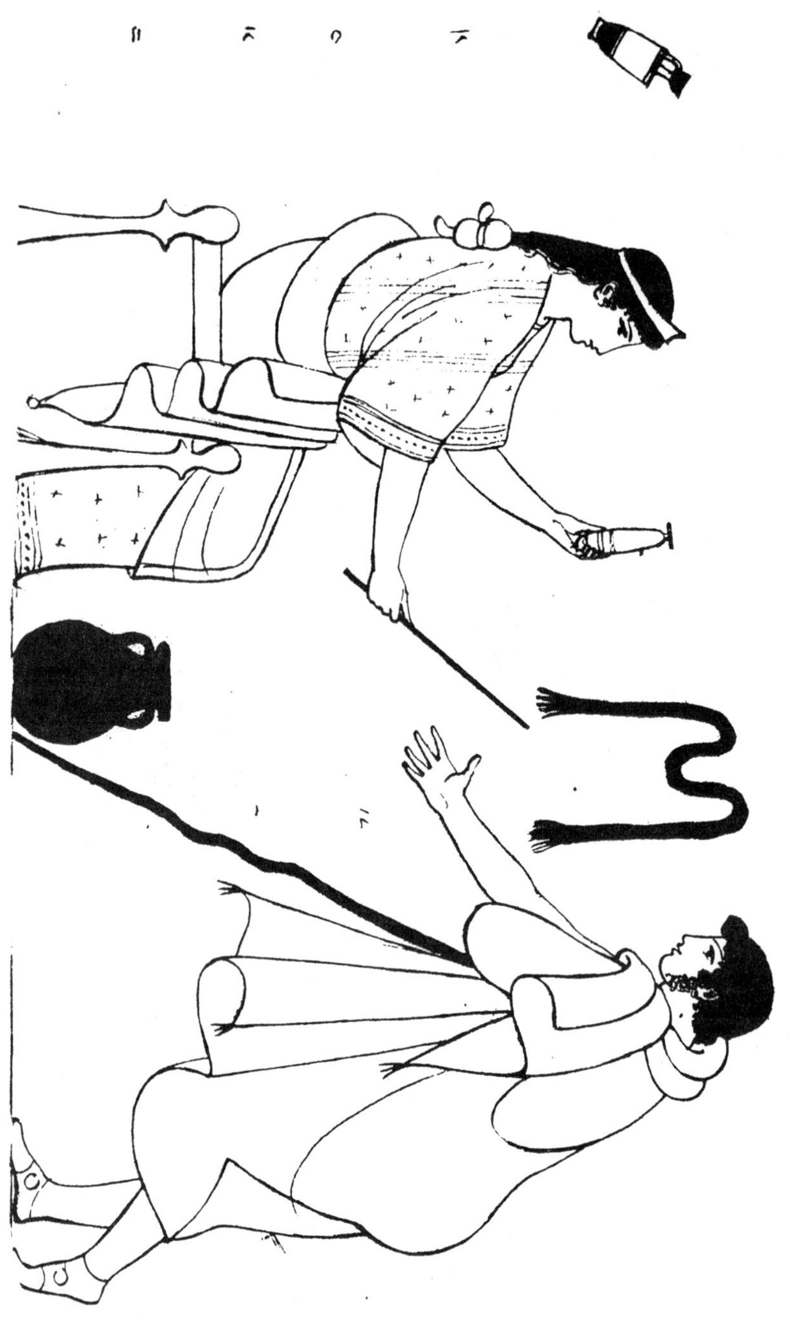

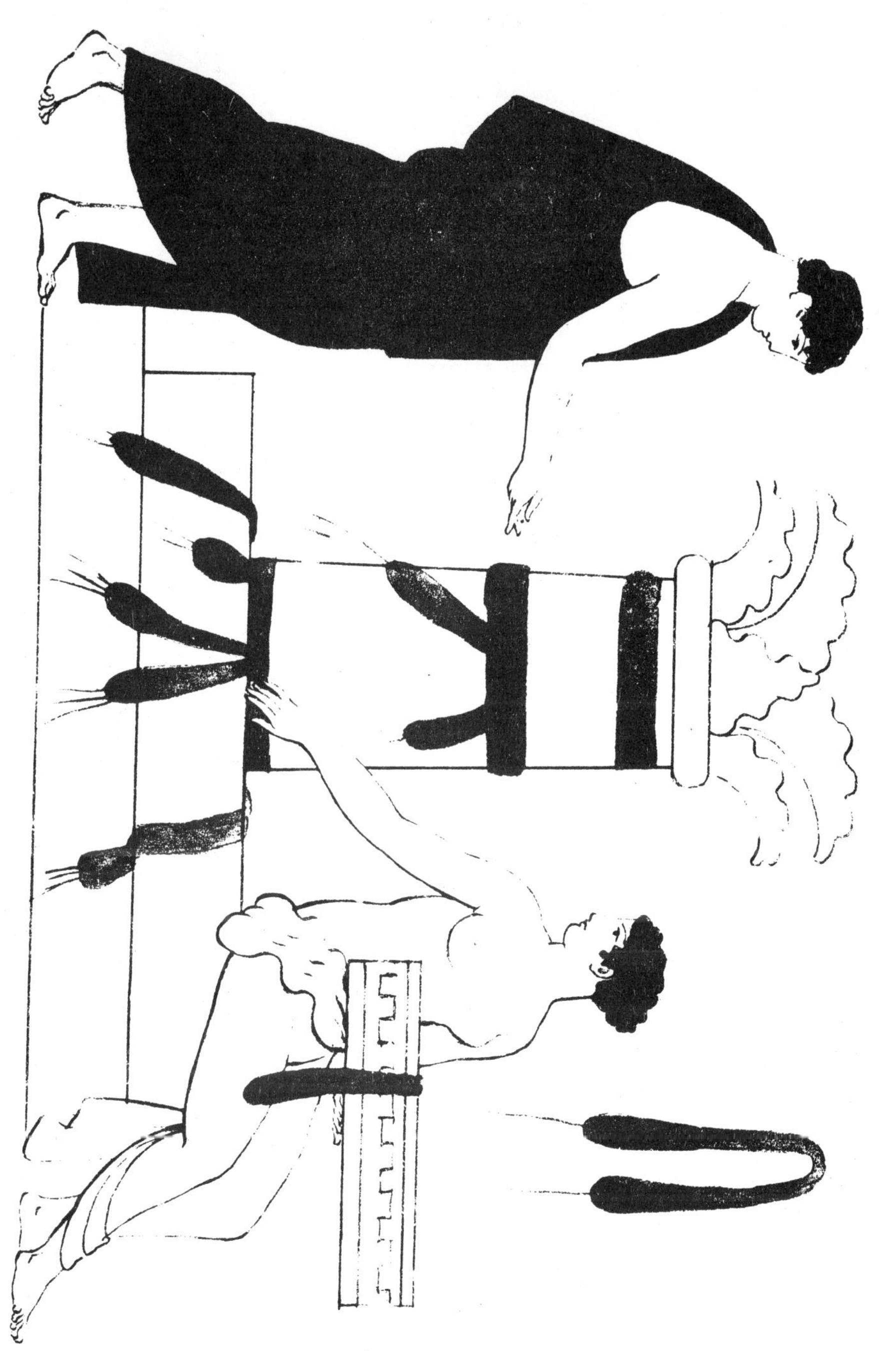

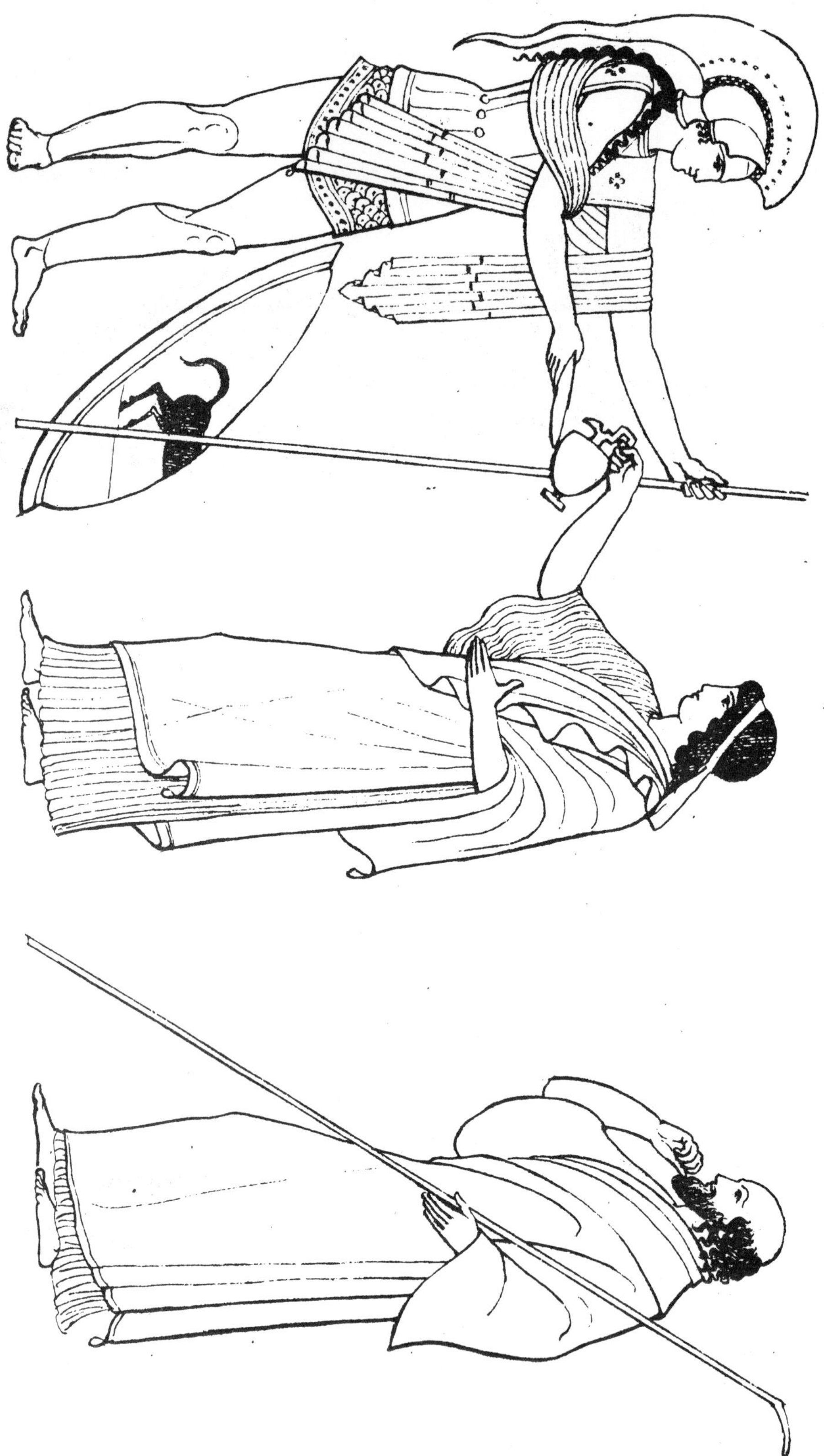

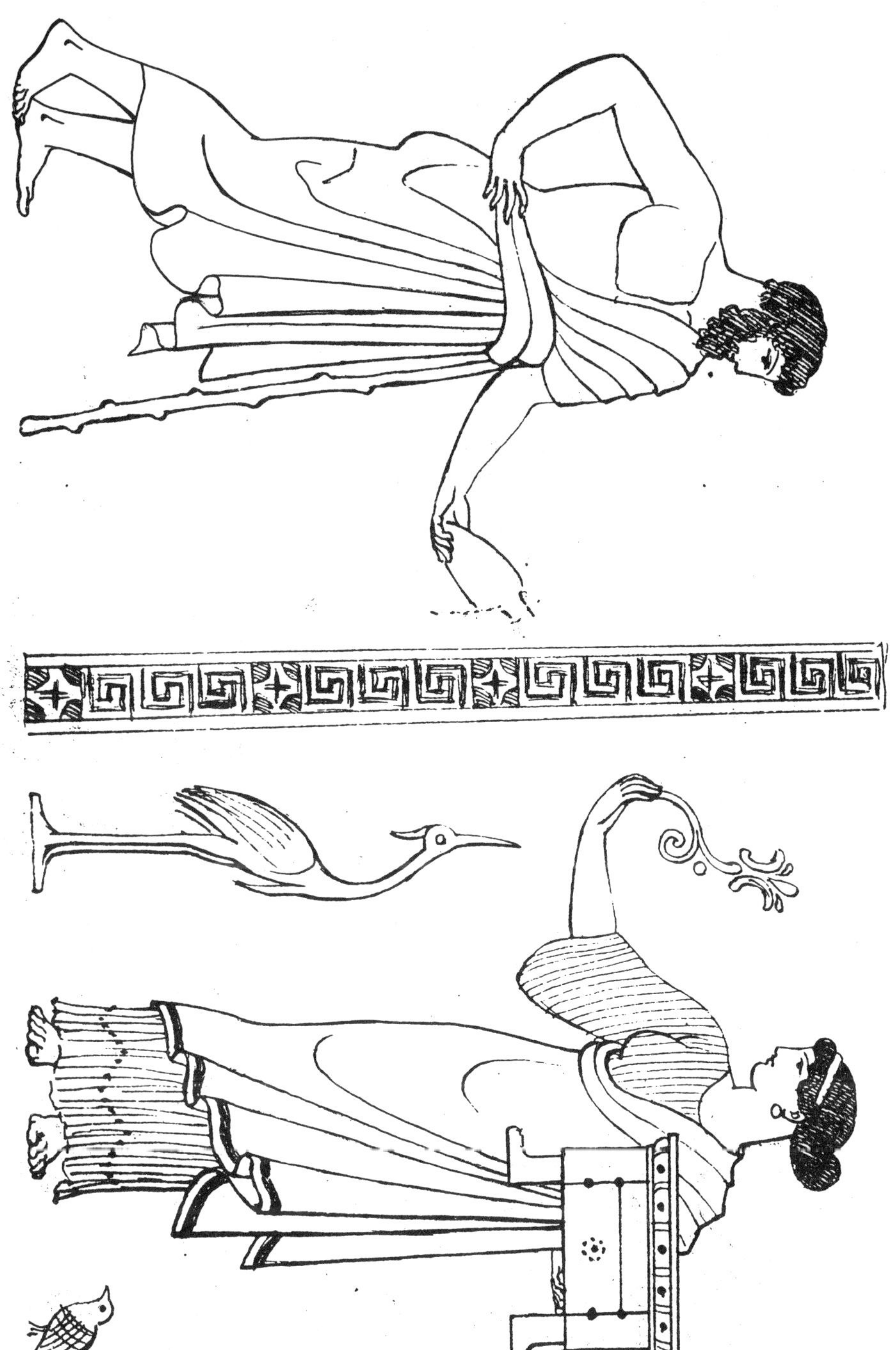

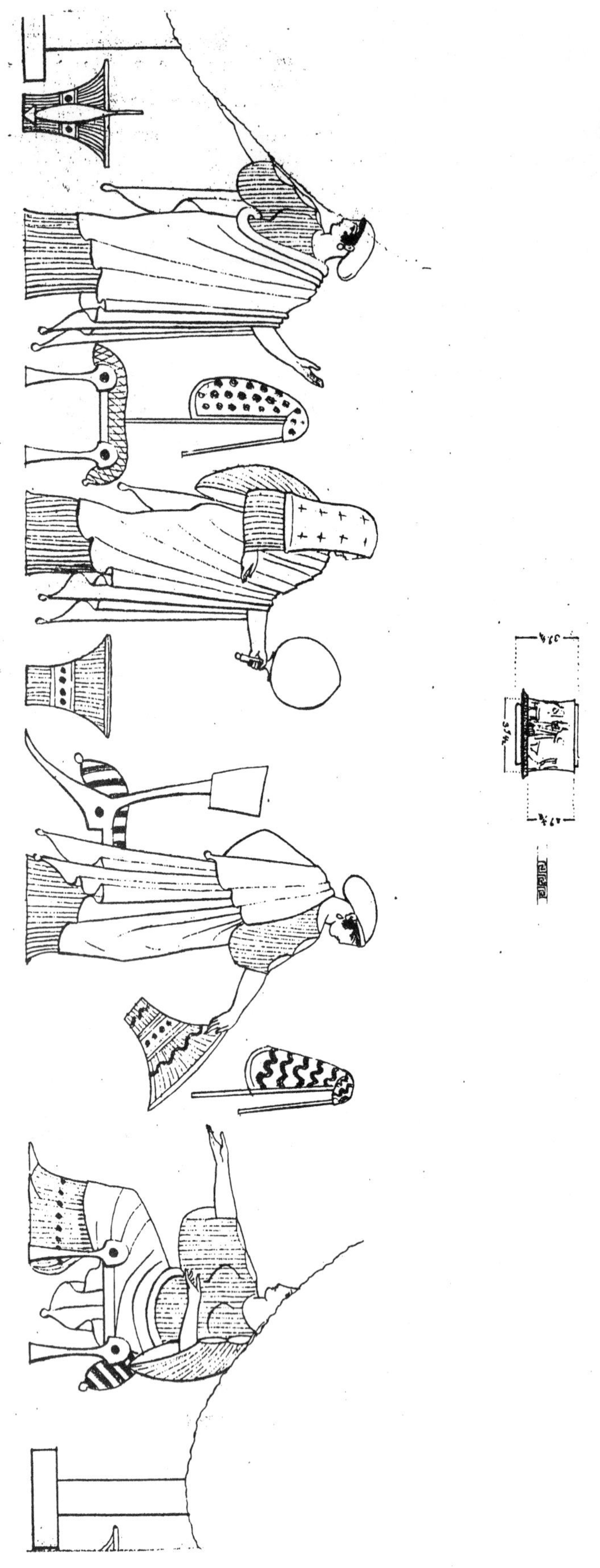

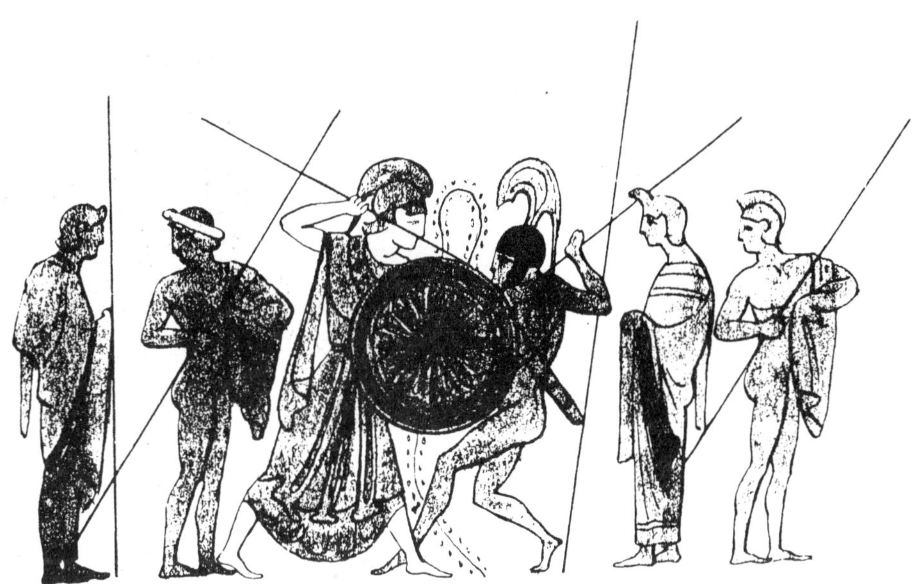

64:72

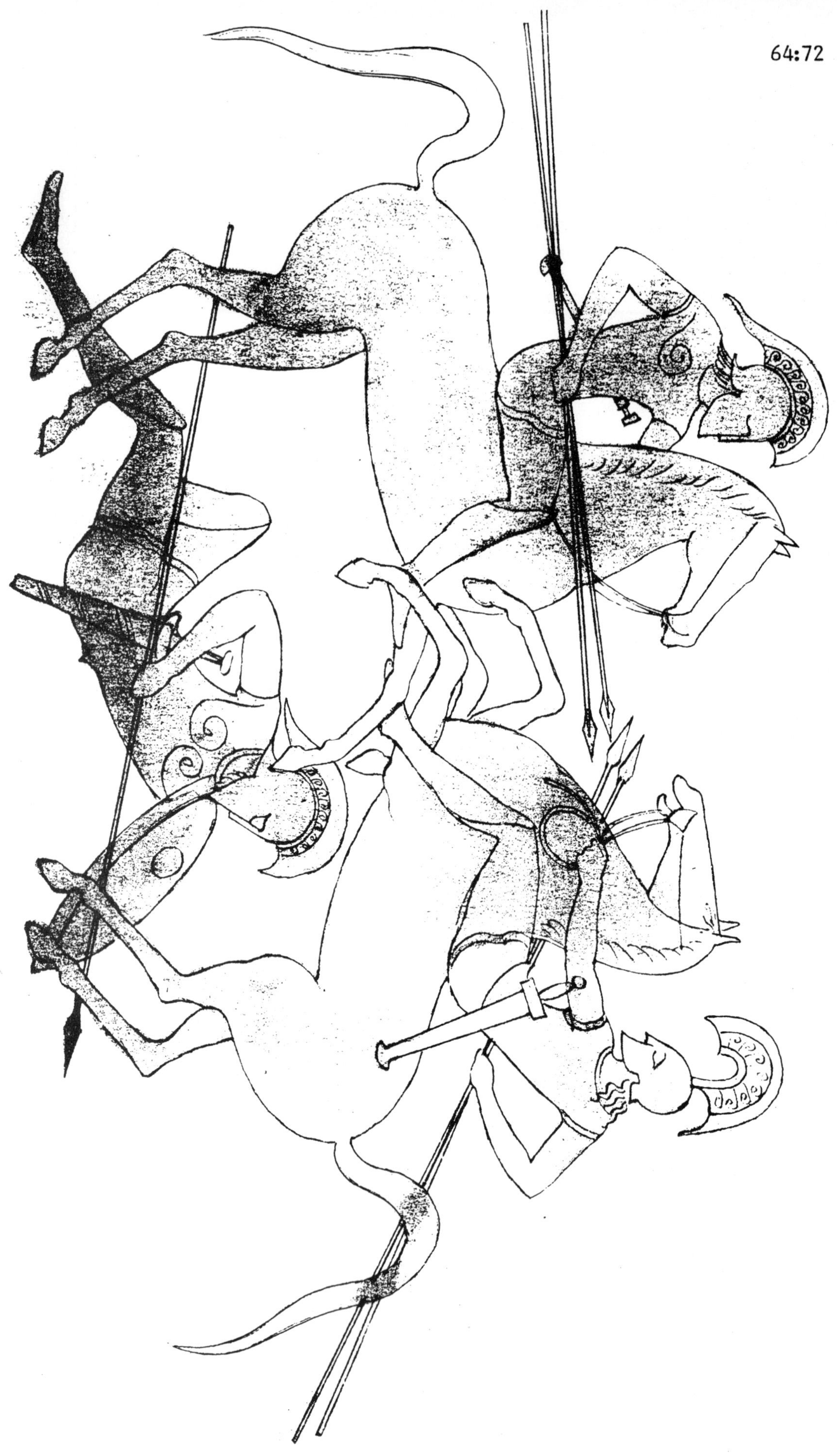

65:73

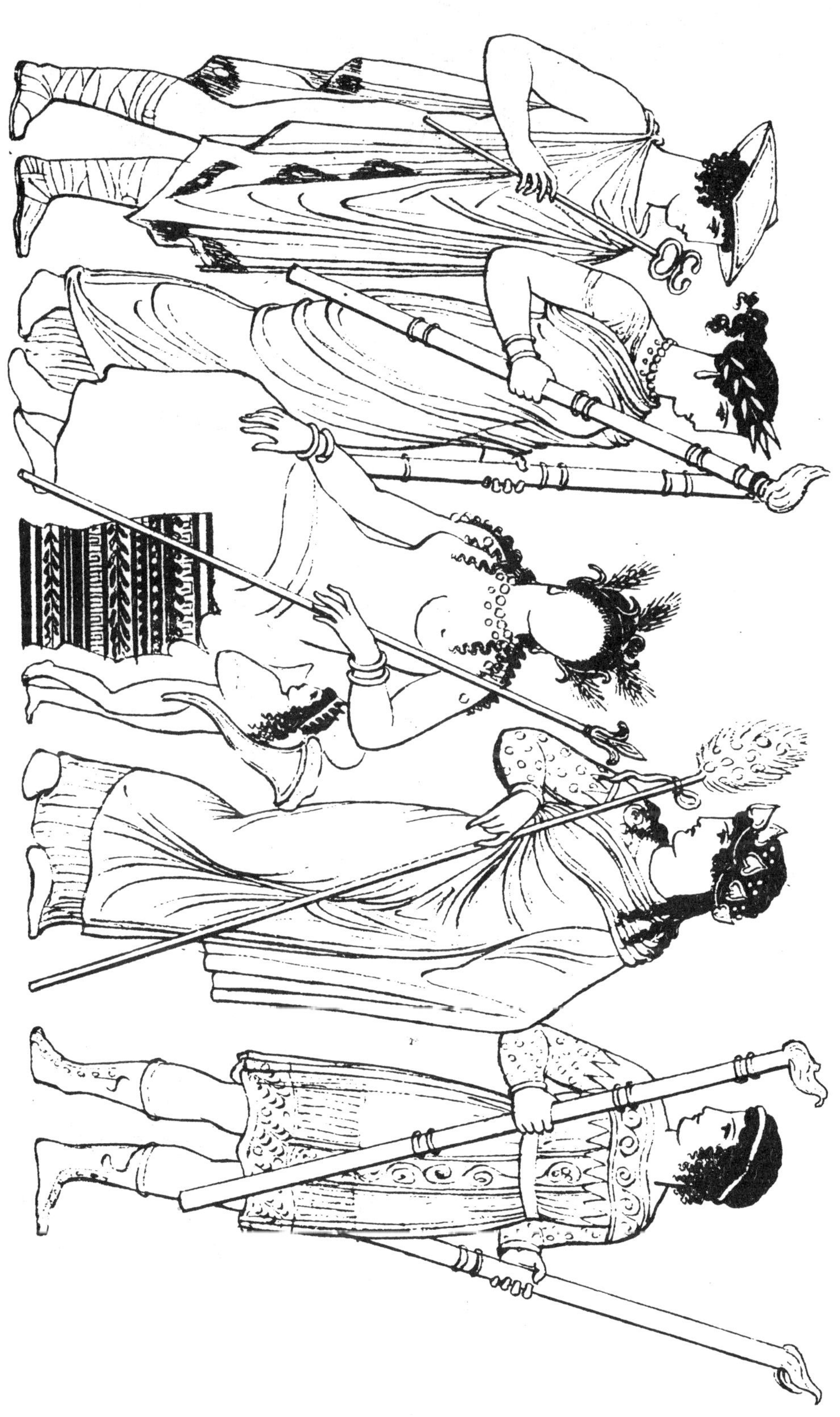

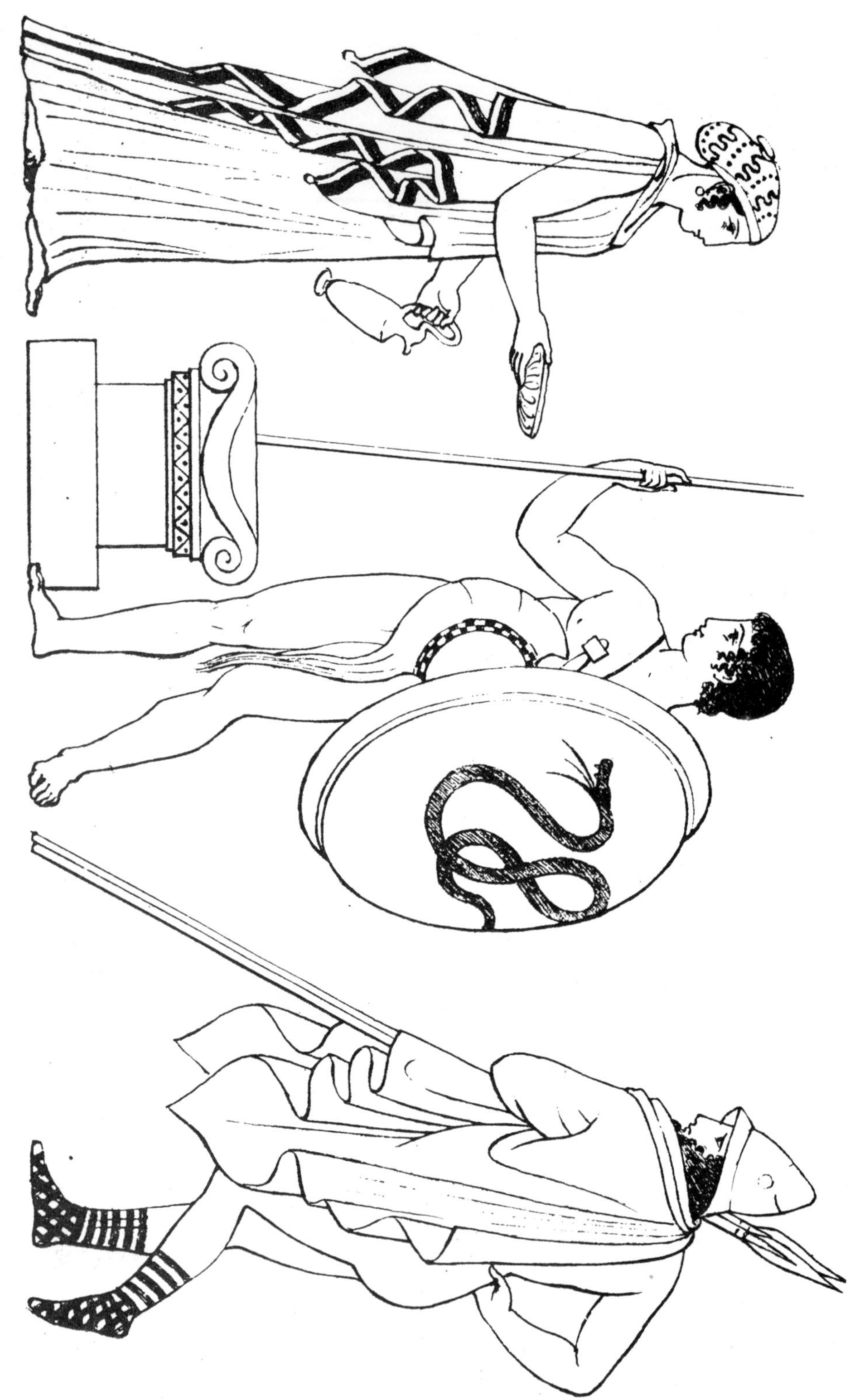

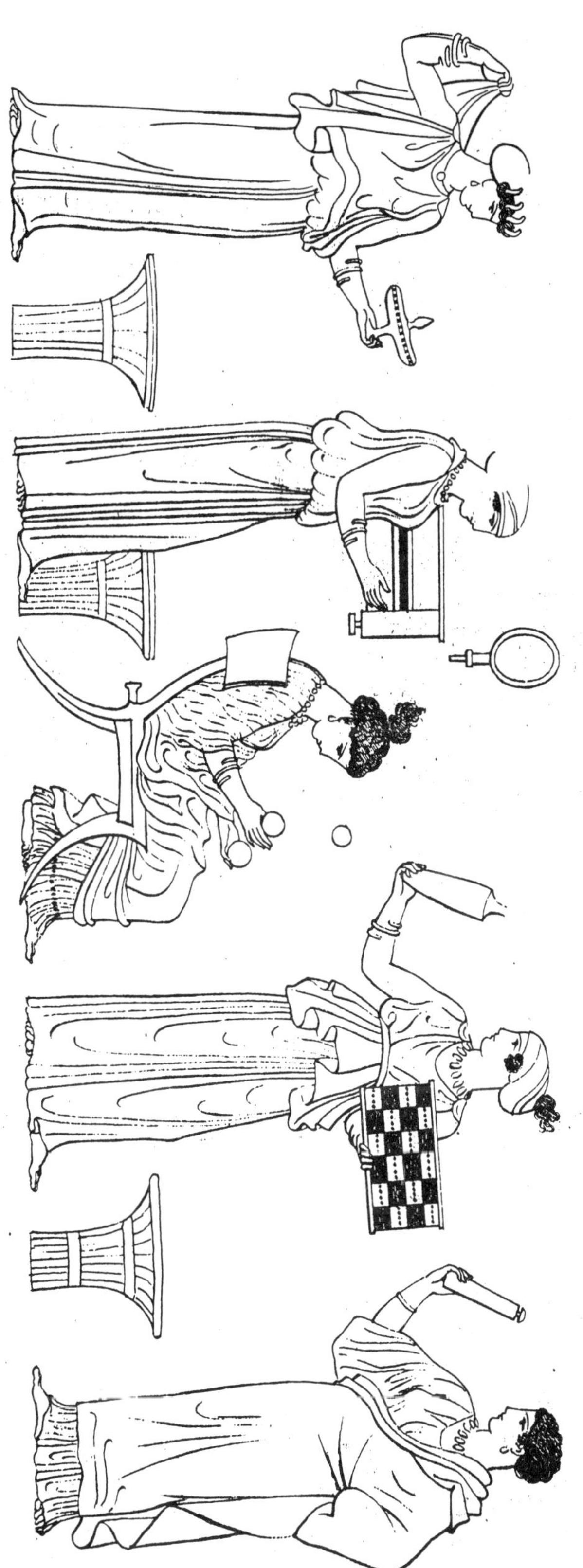

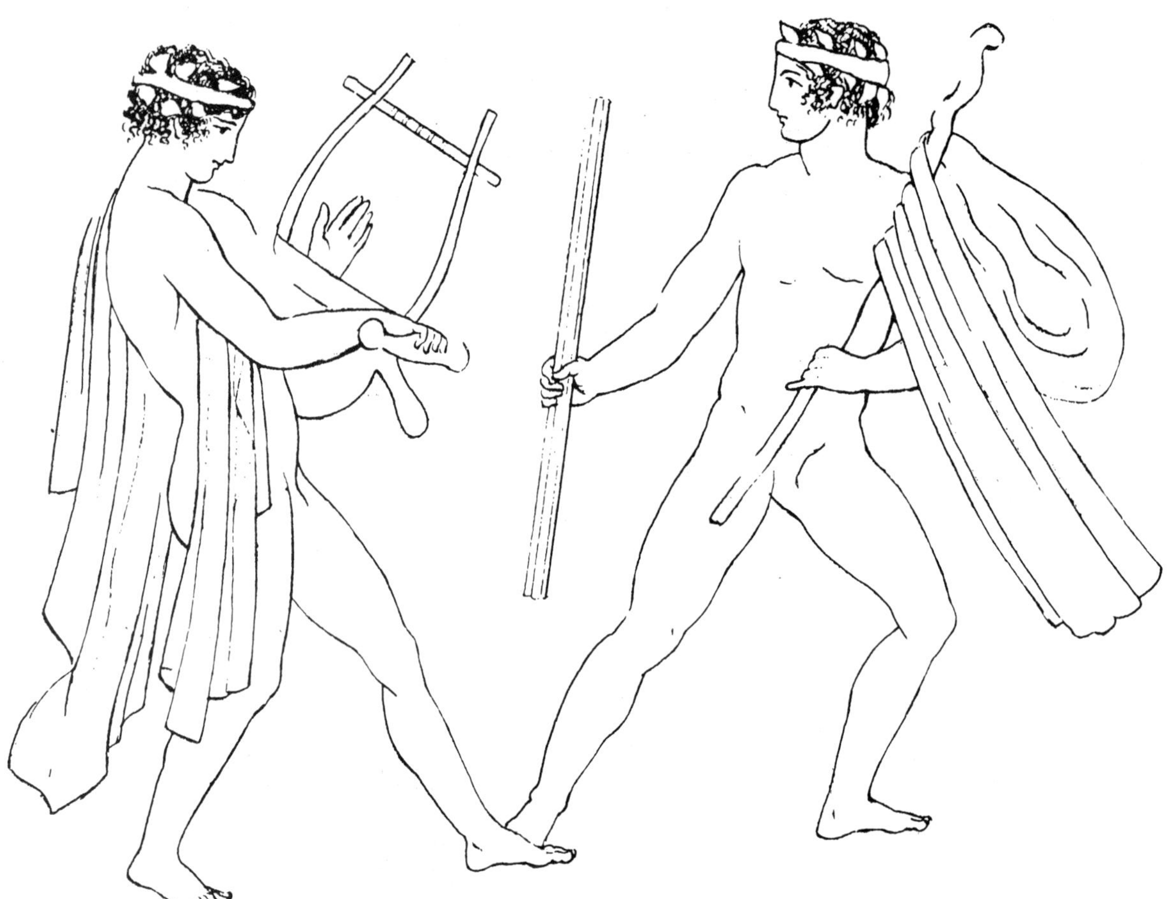

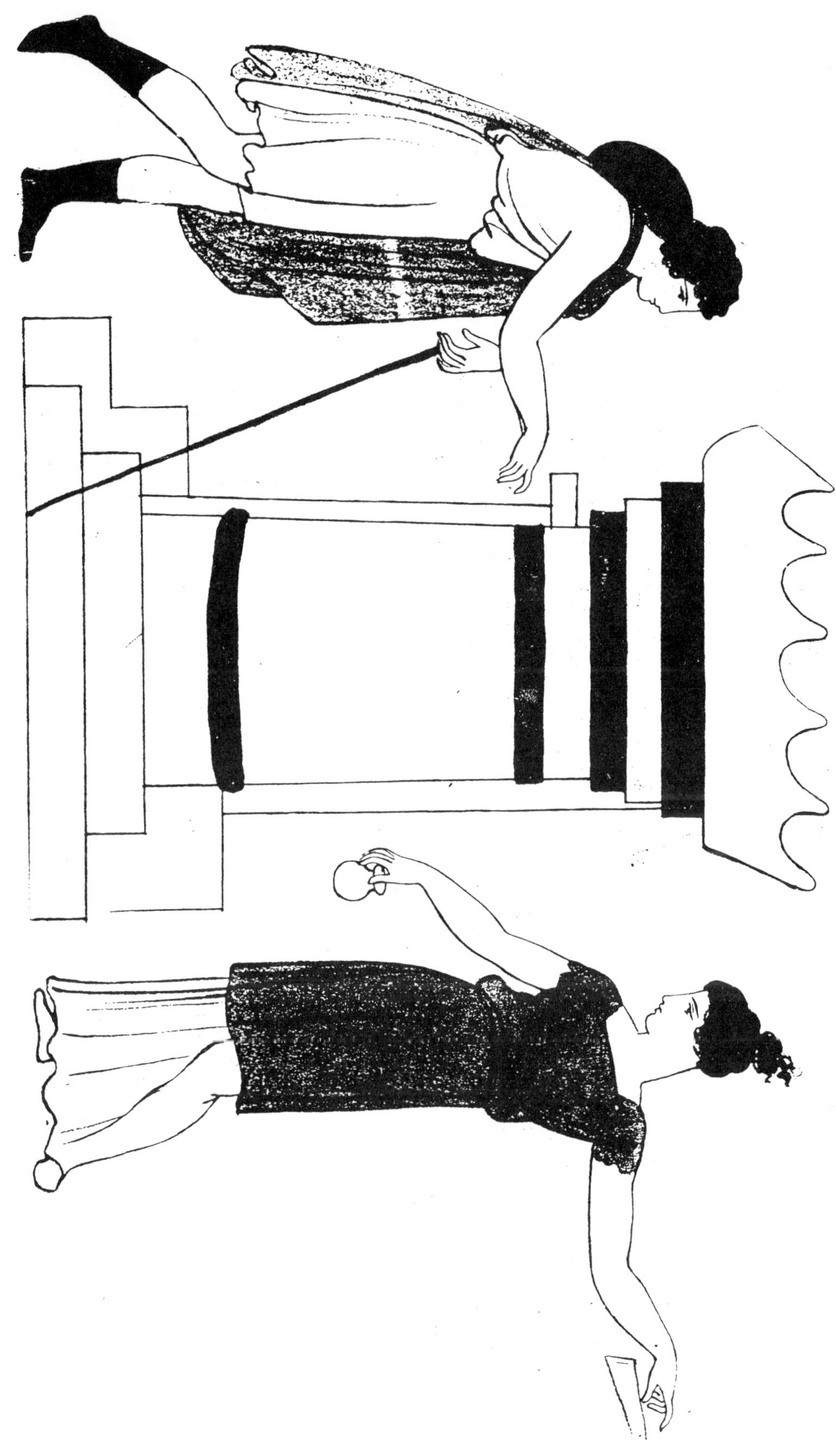

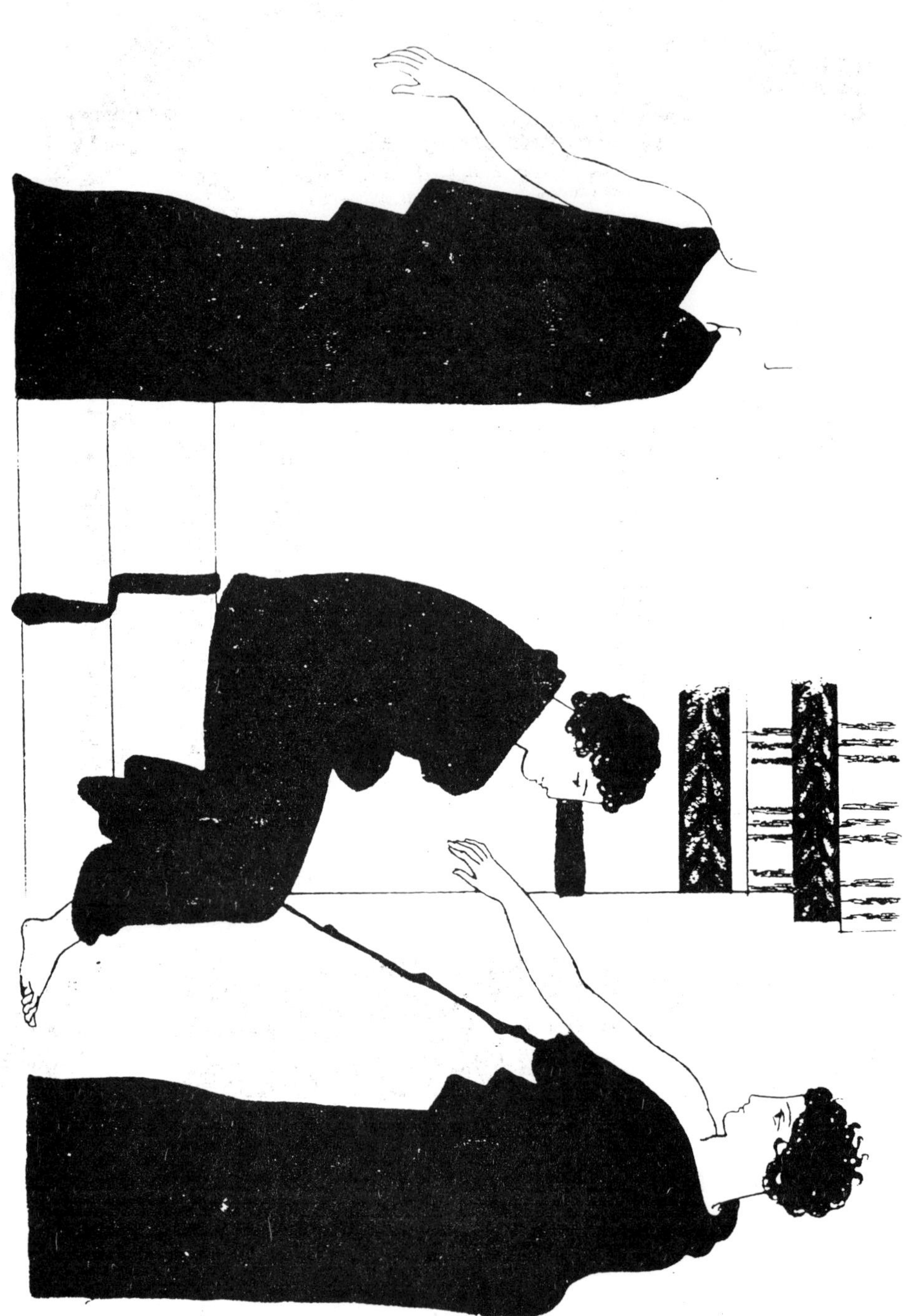

68:79

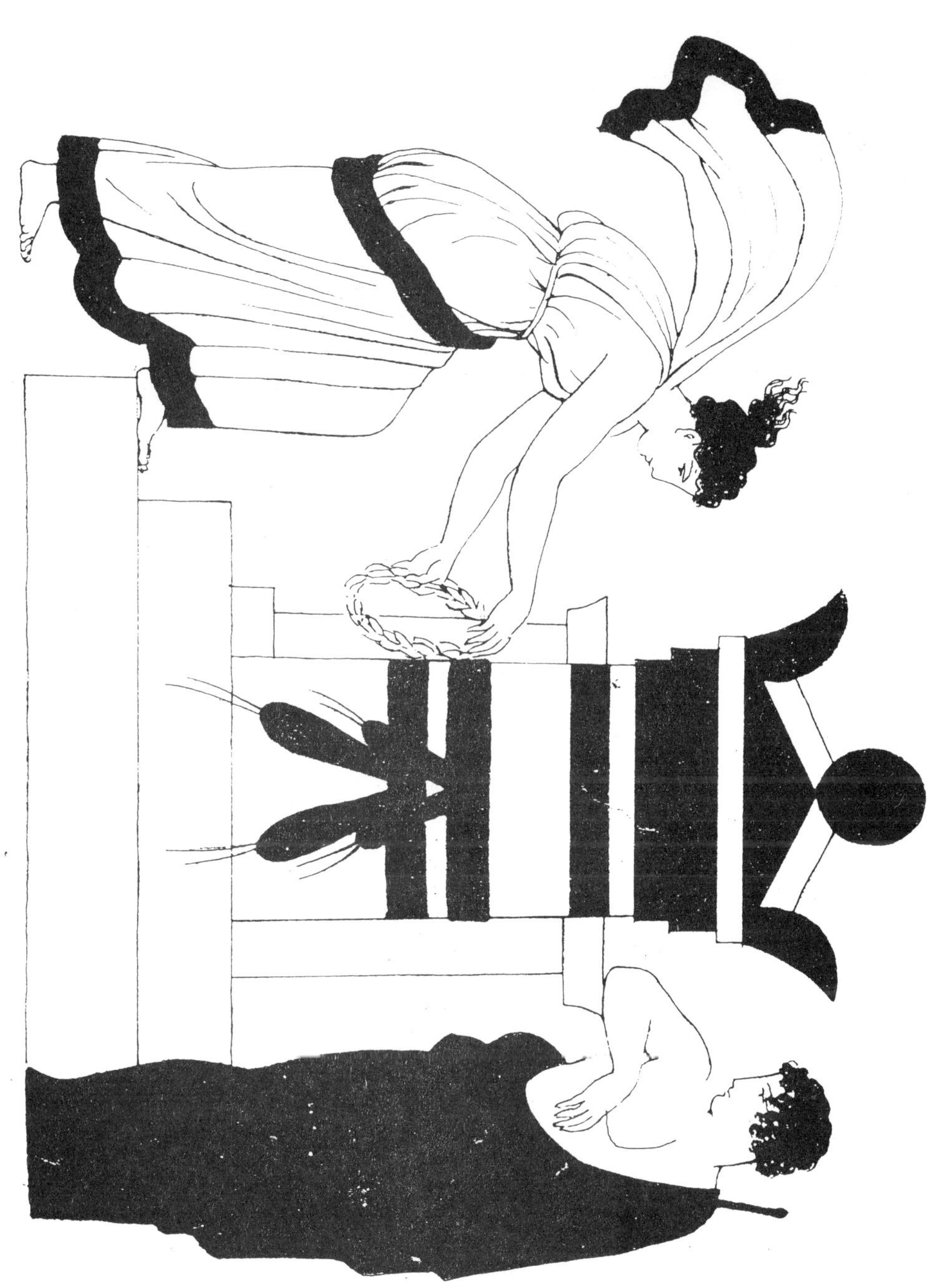

69:80

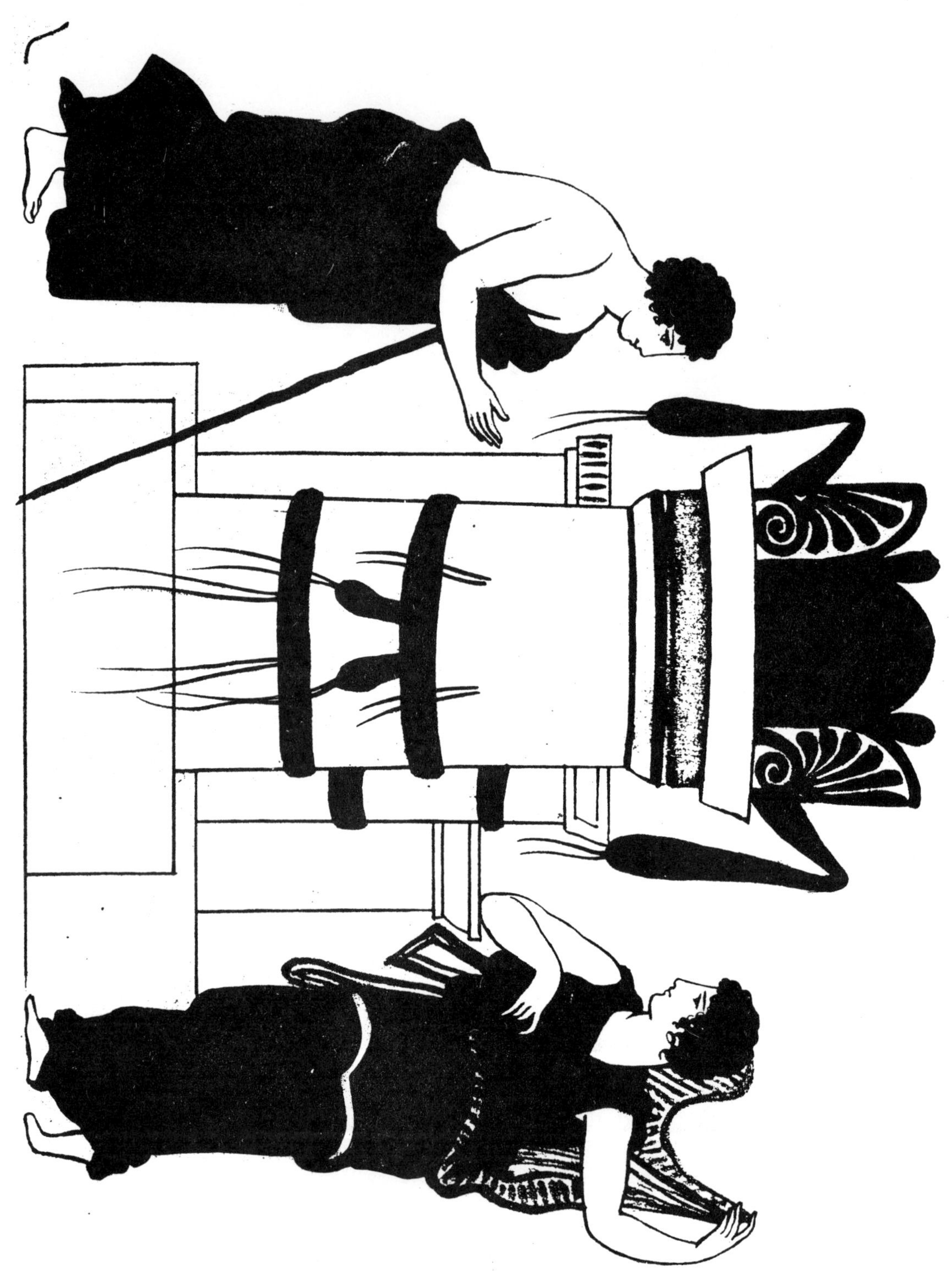

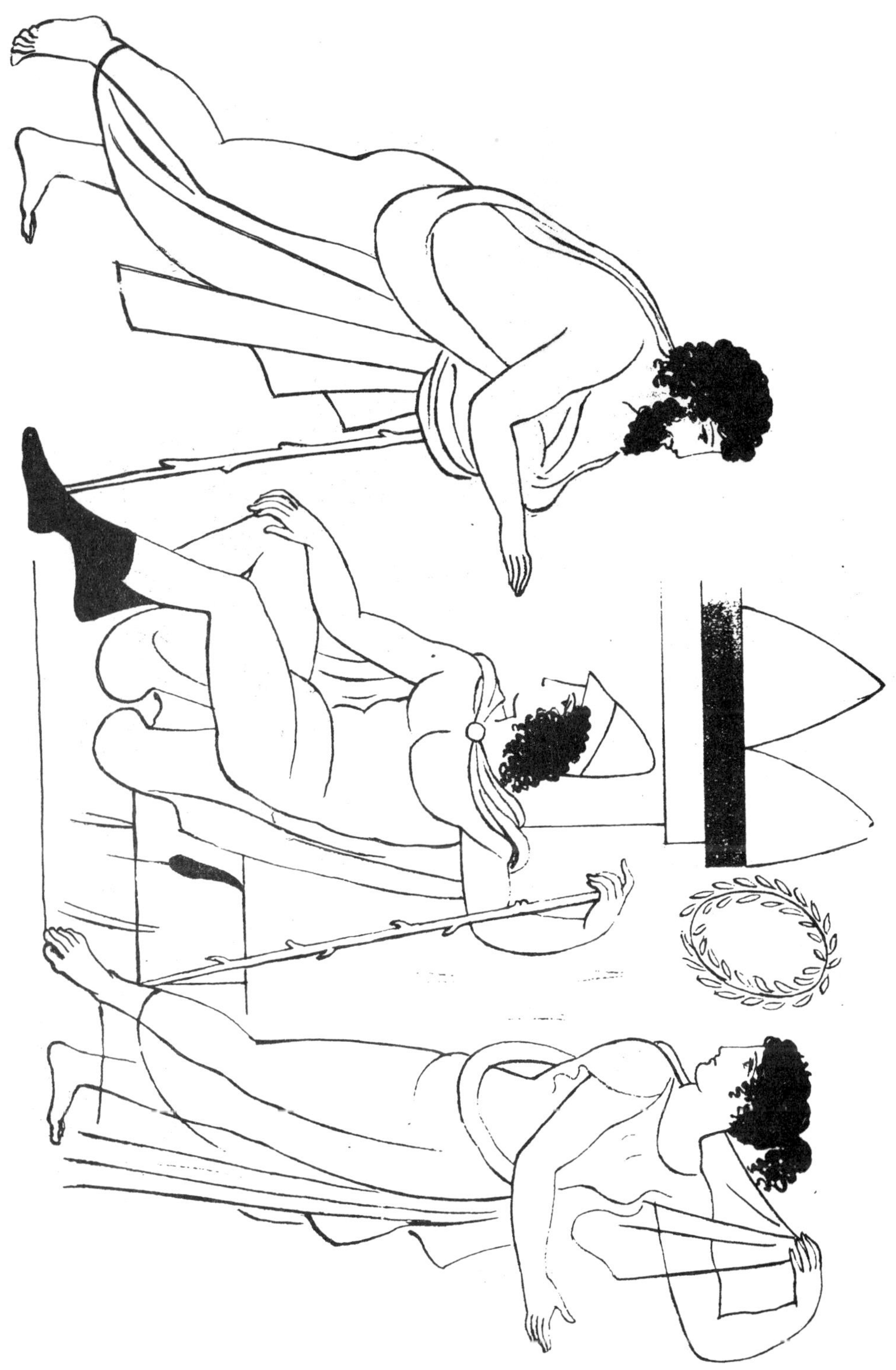

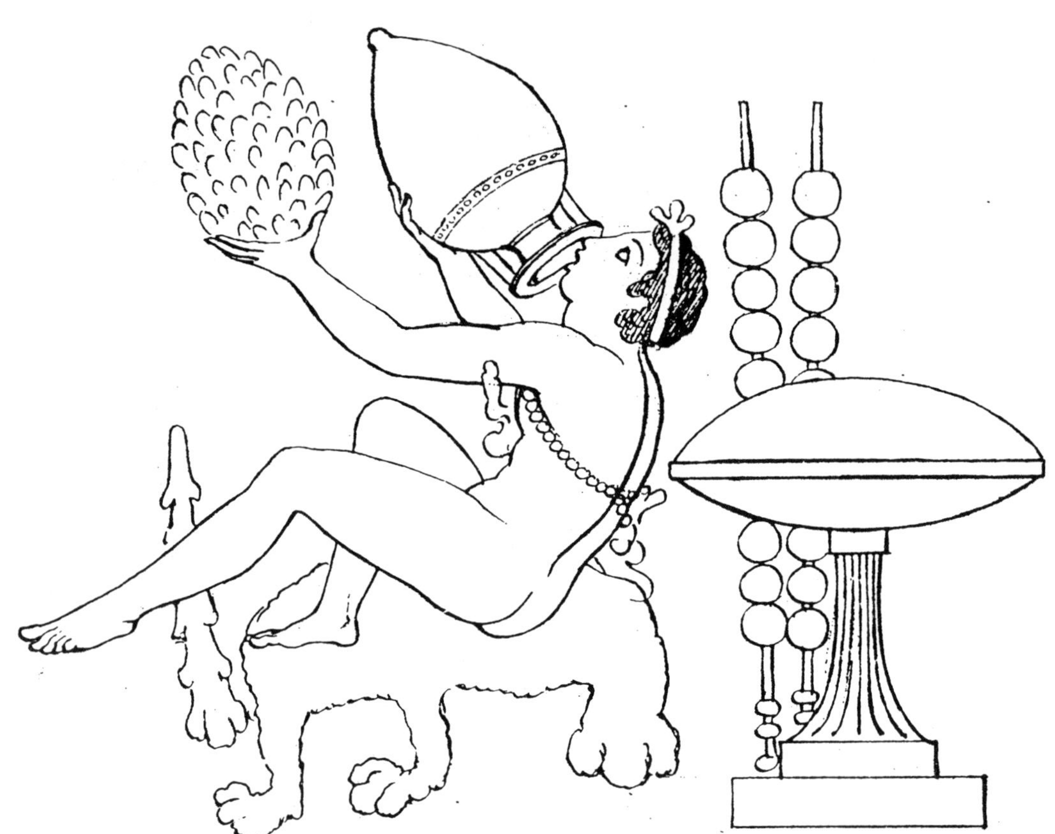

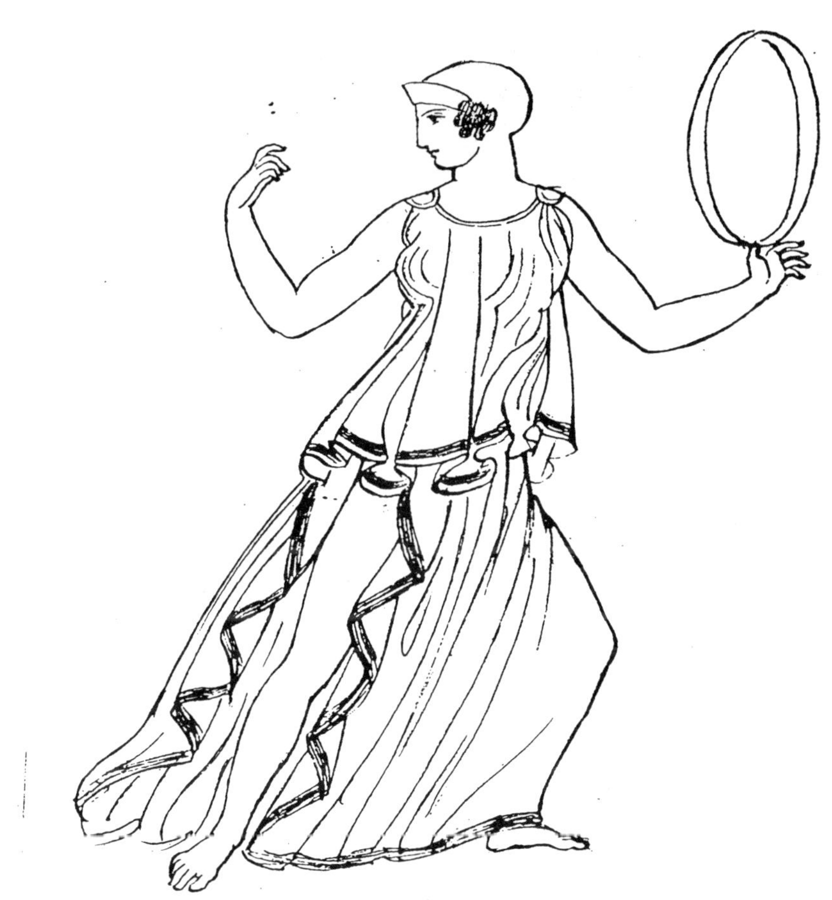

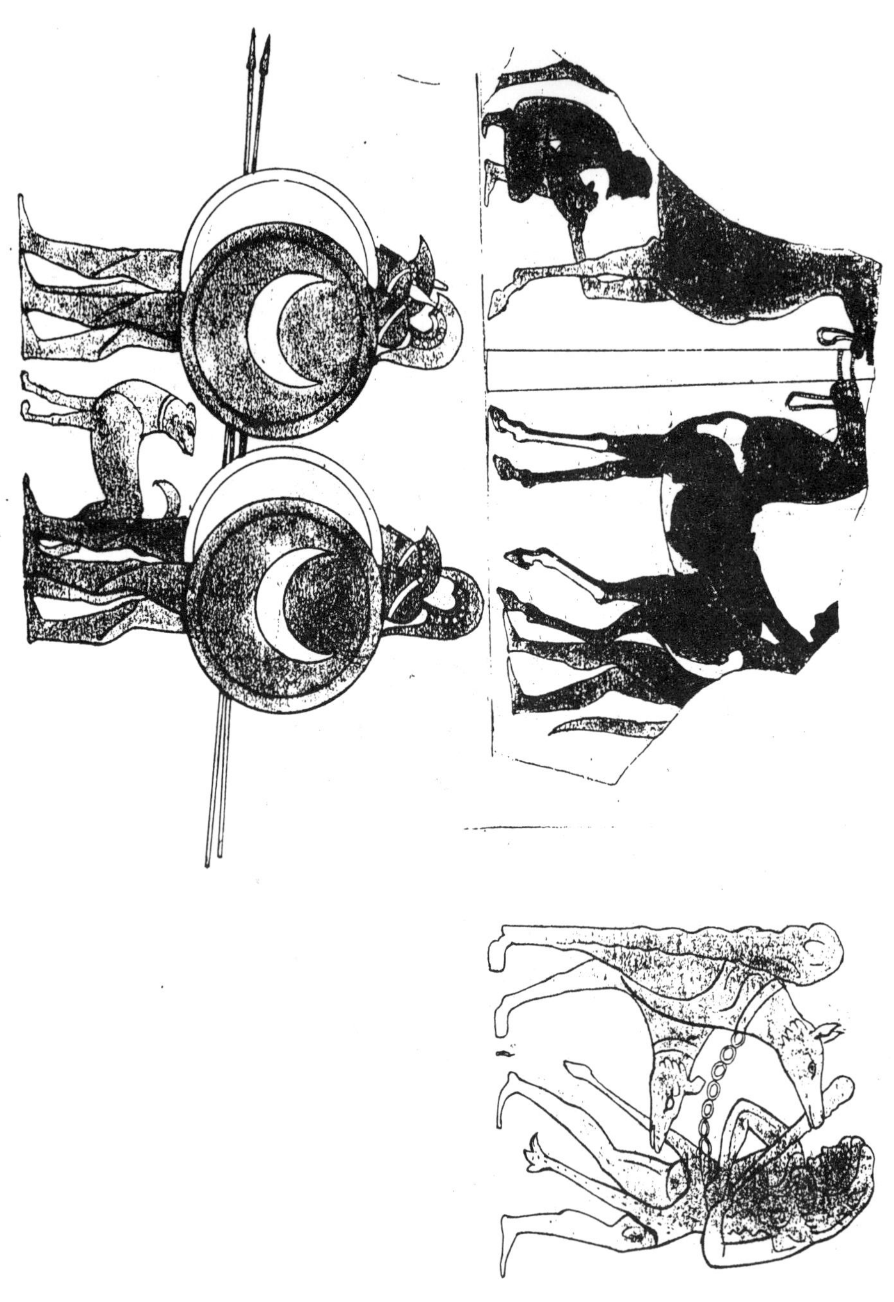

72:84 and 85

72:86(i), (ii) and (iii)

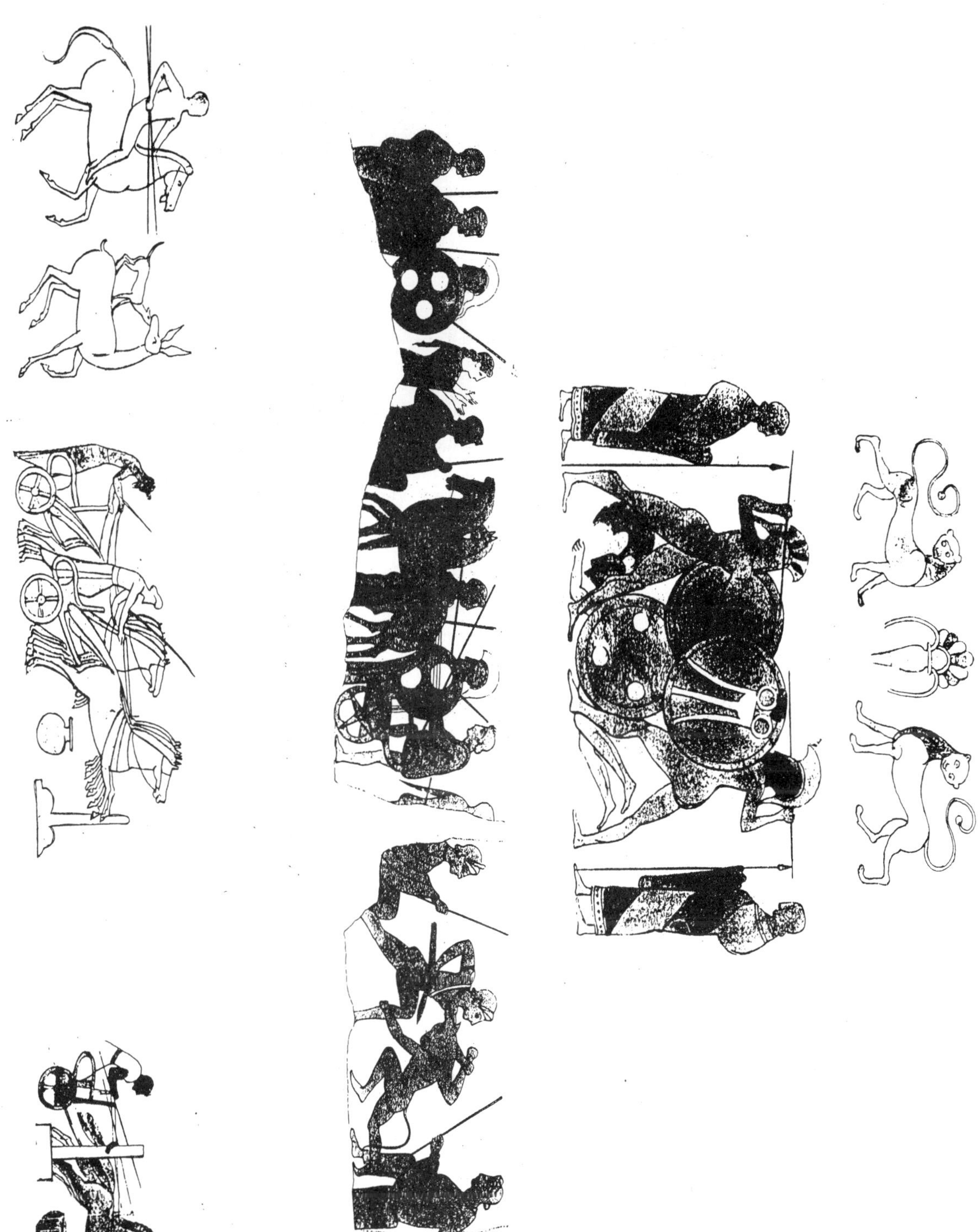

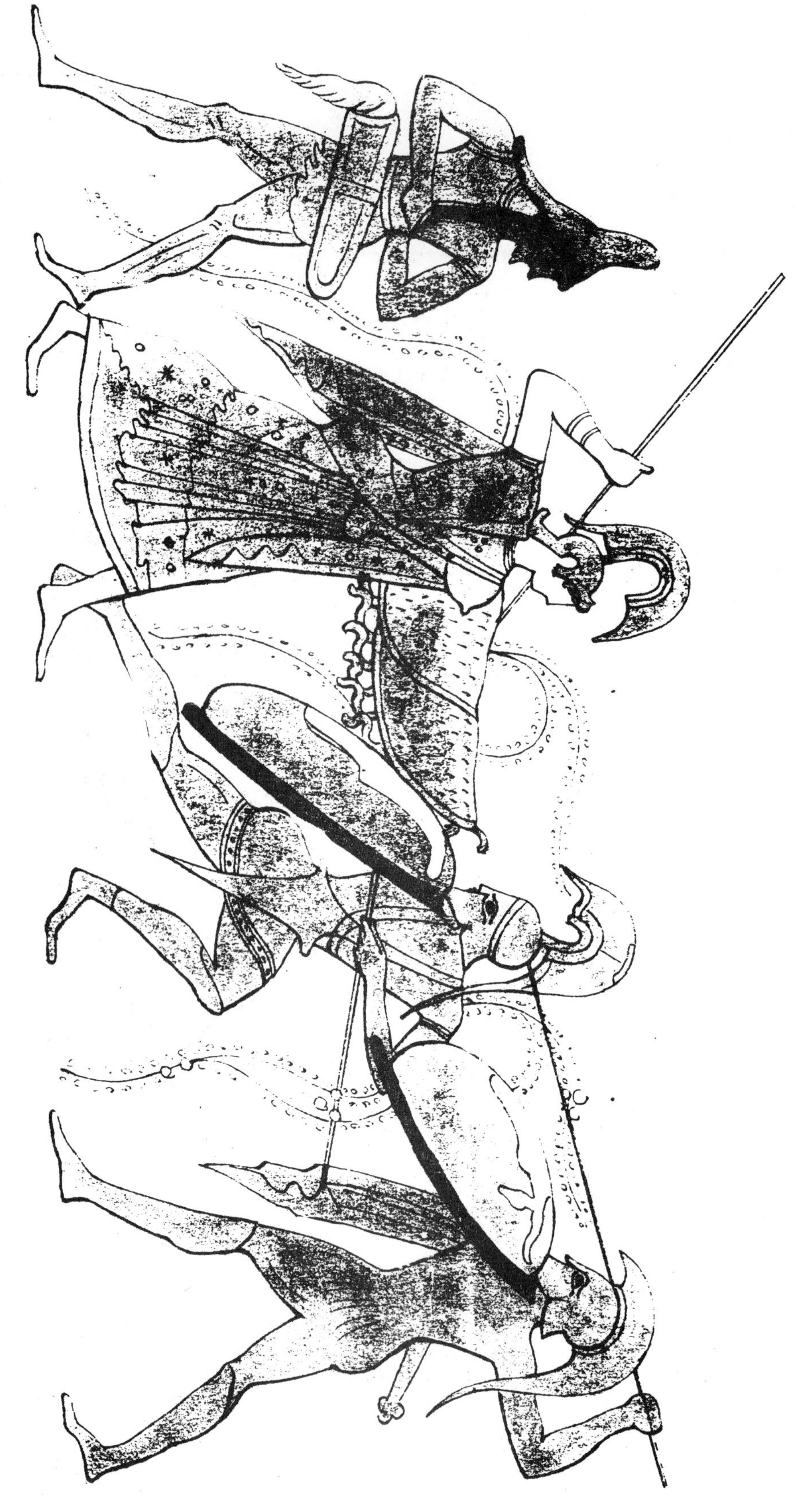

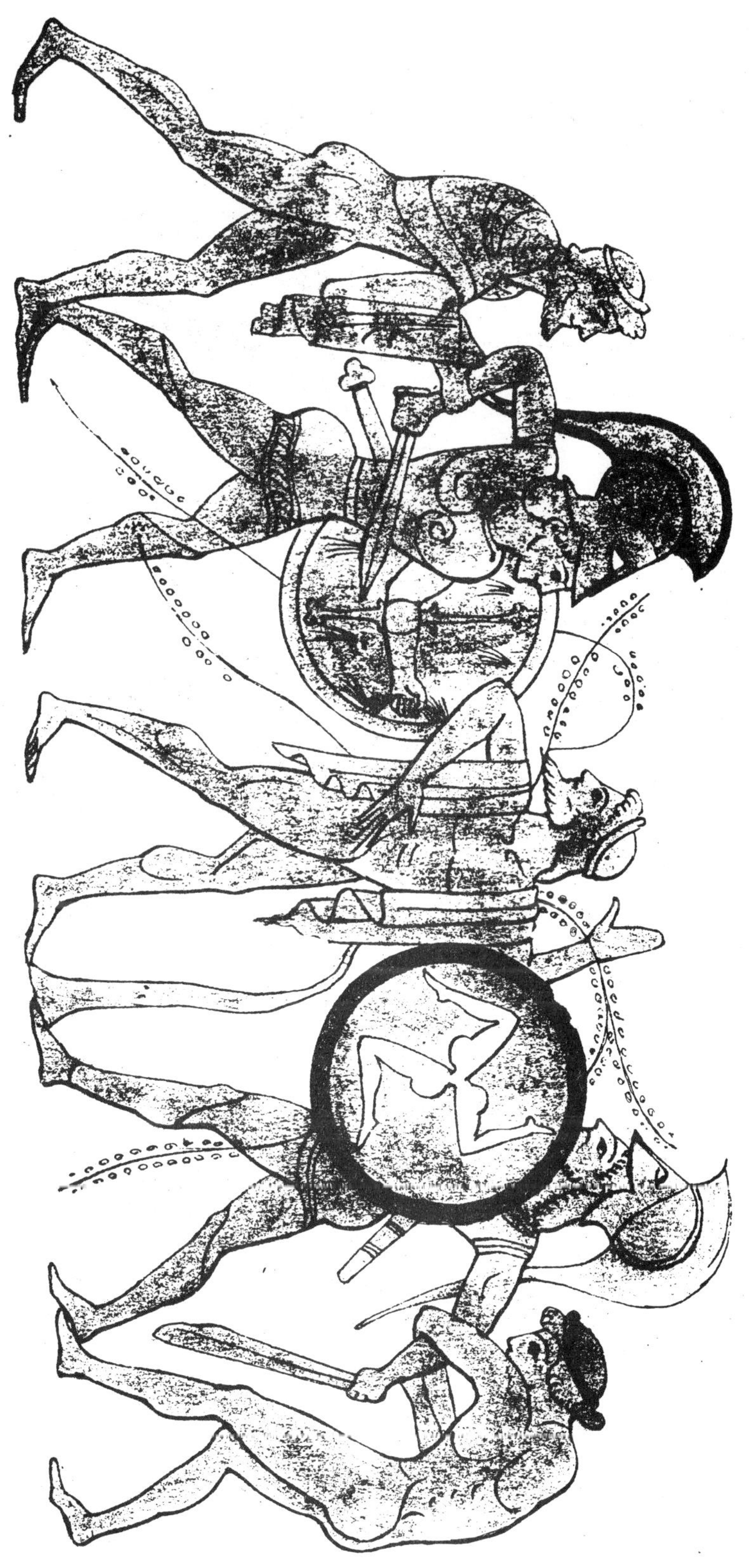

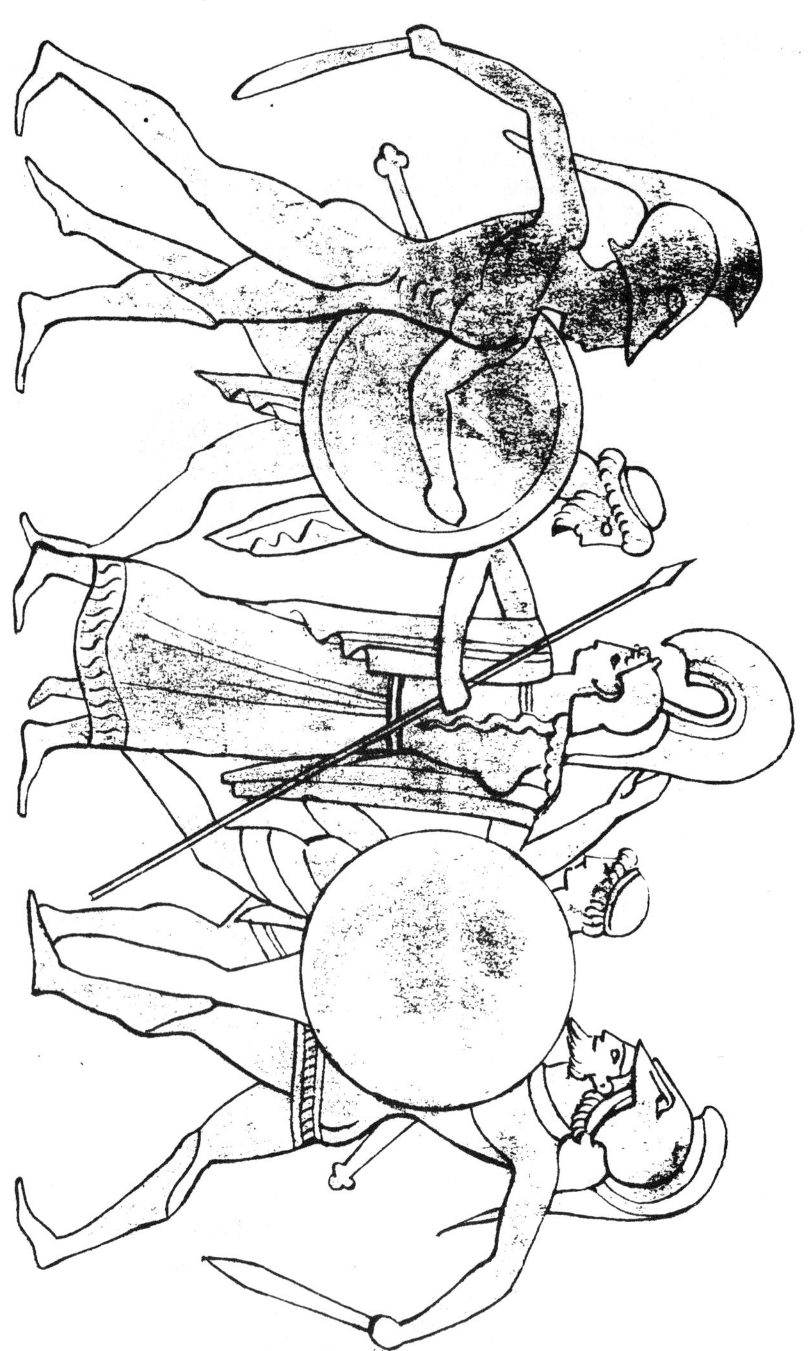

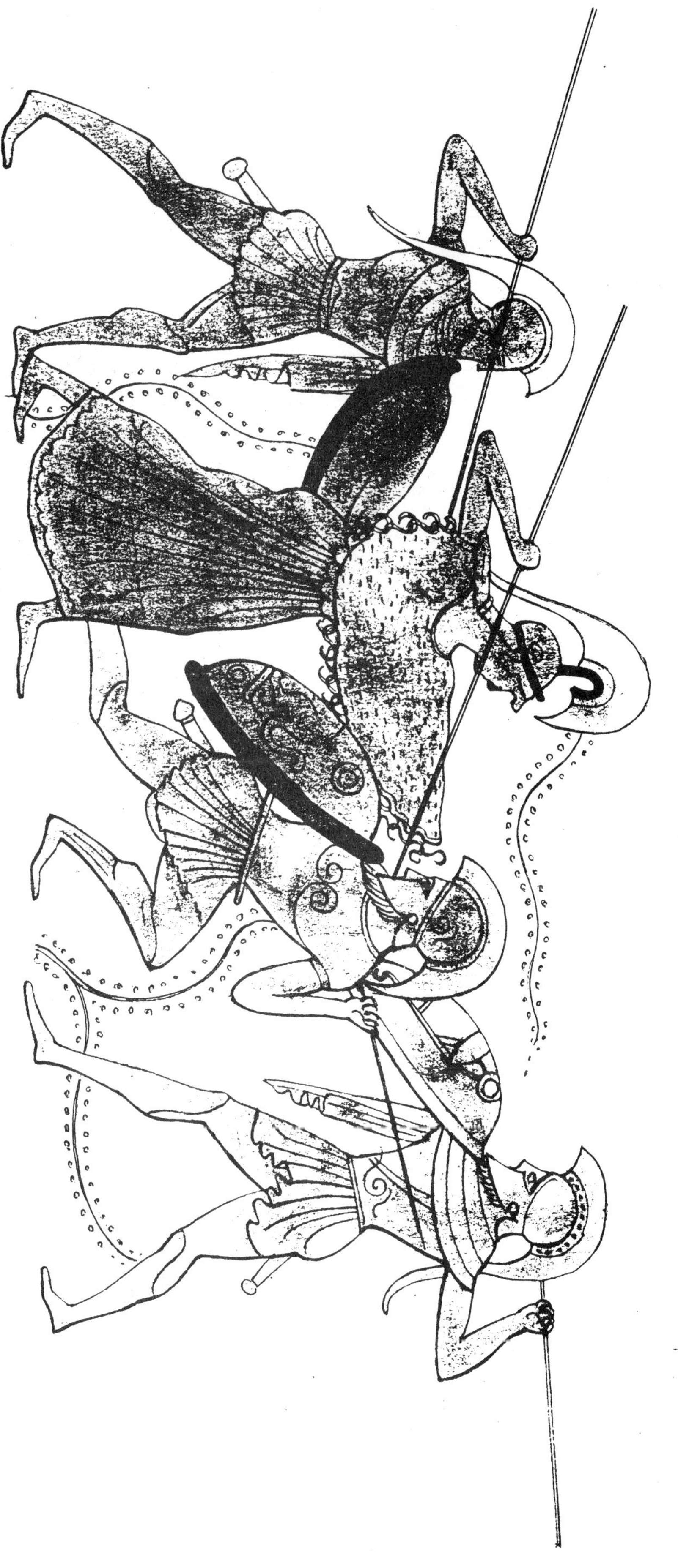

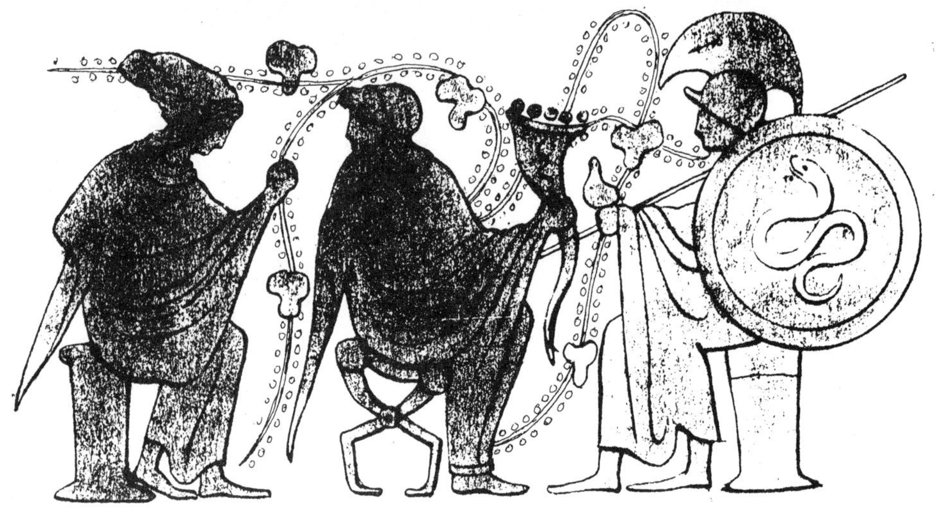

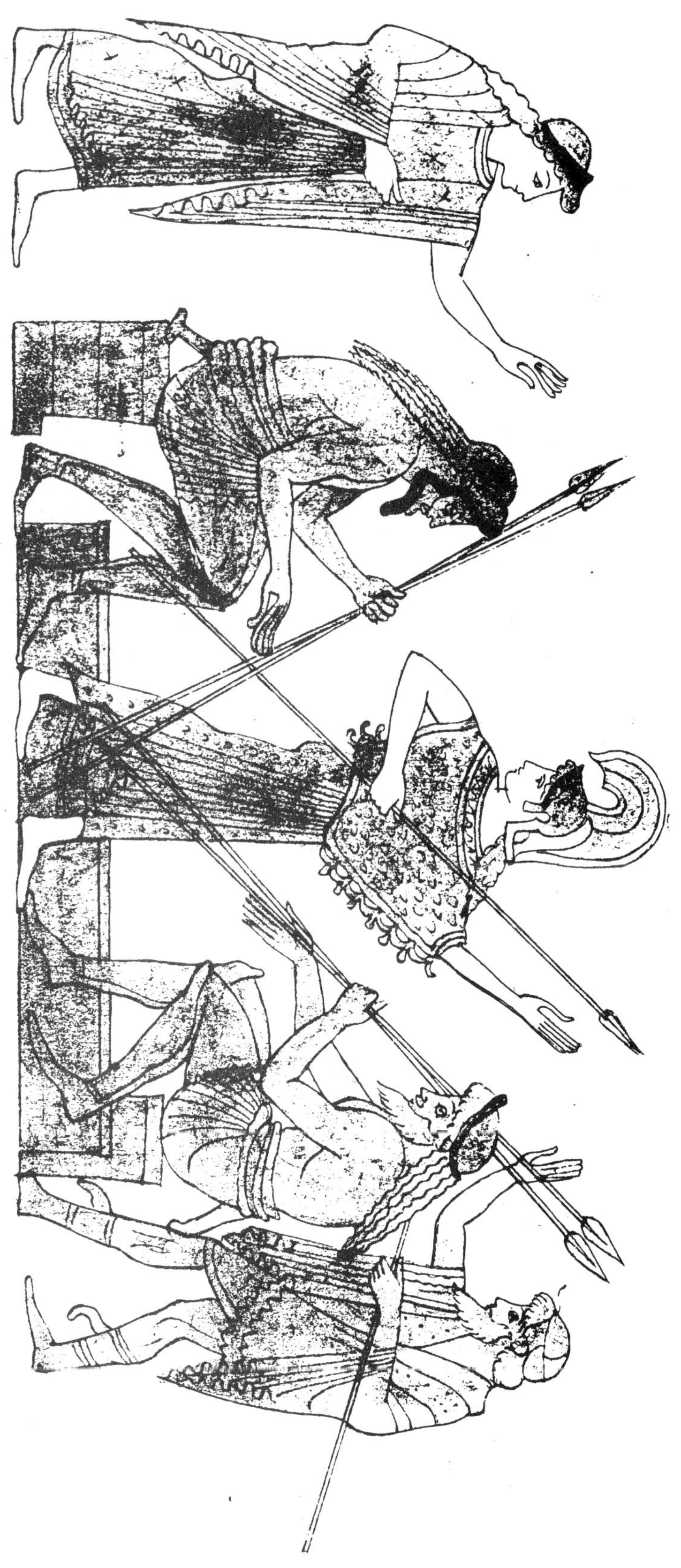

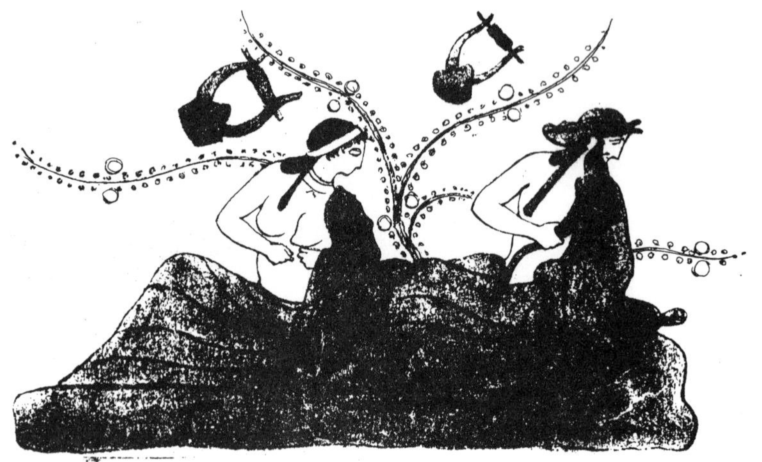

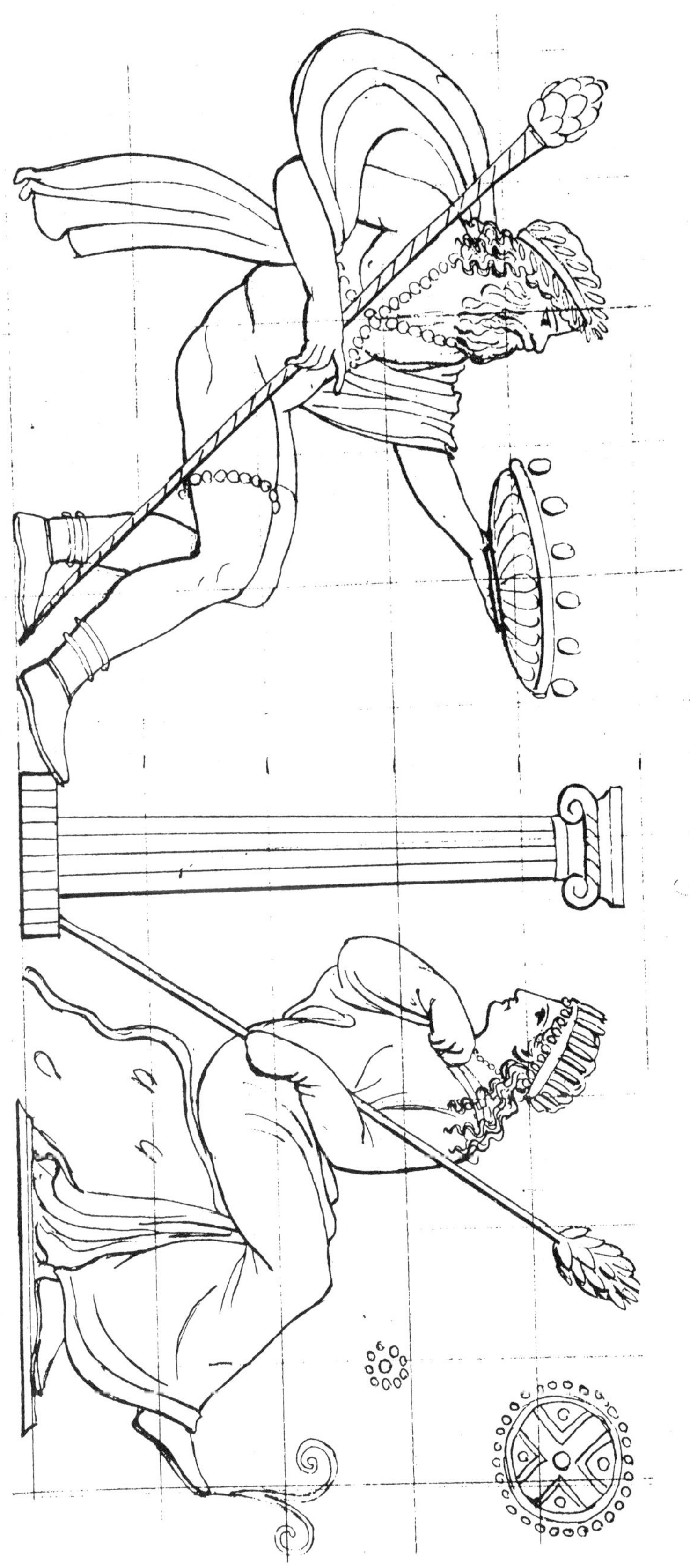

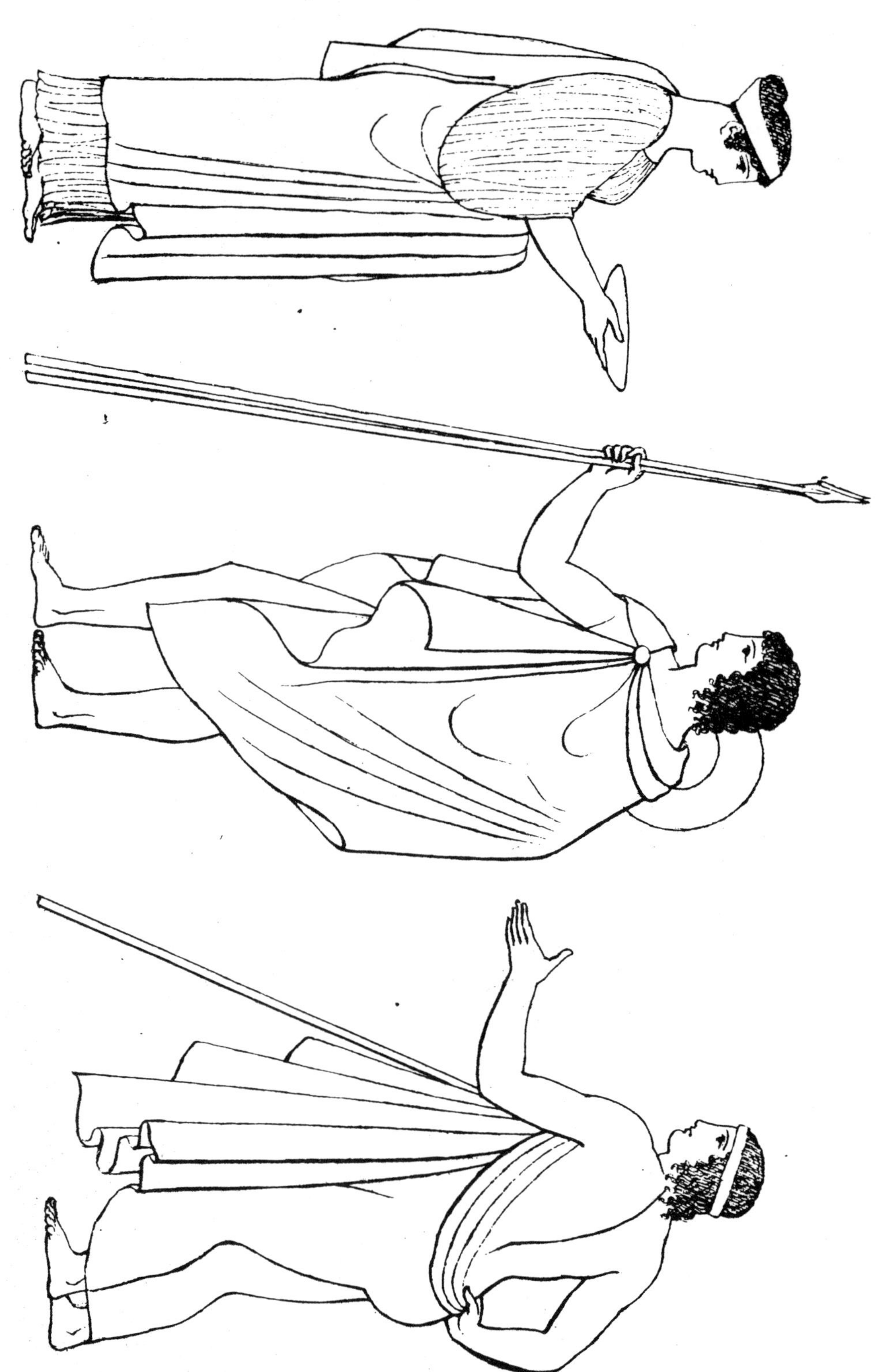

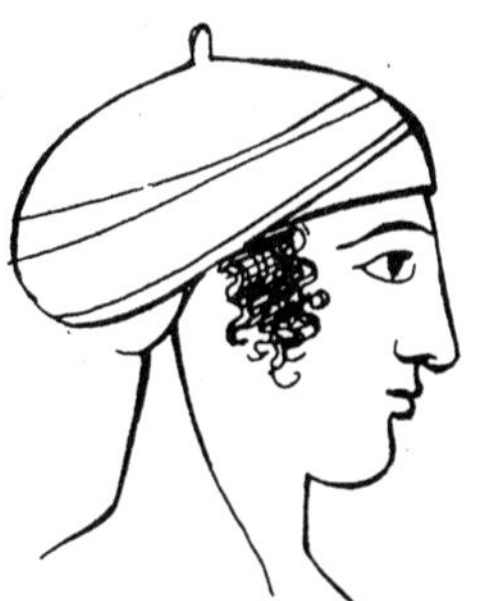

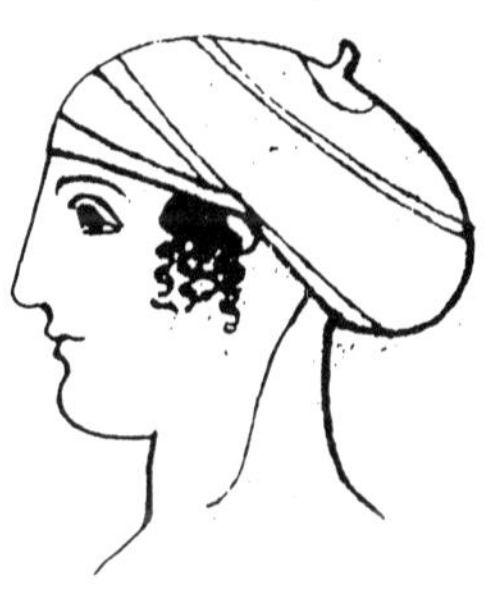

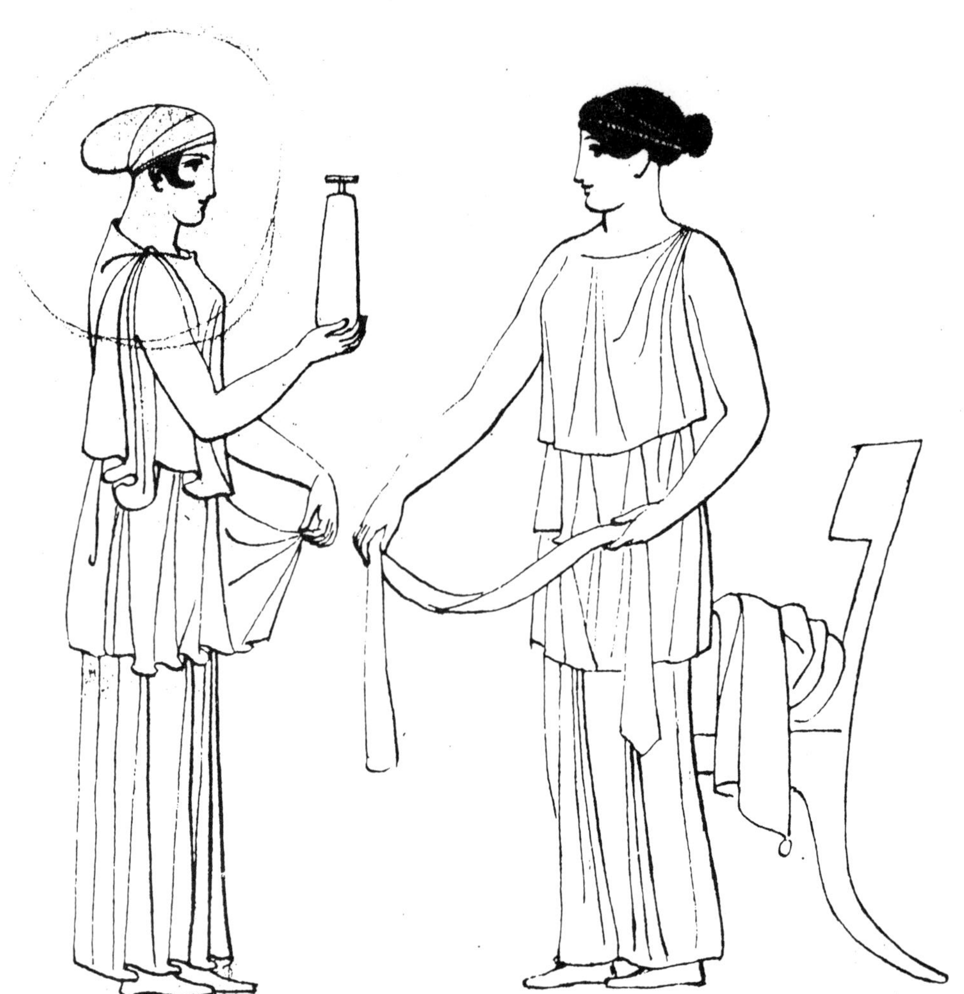

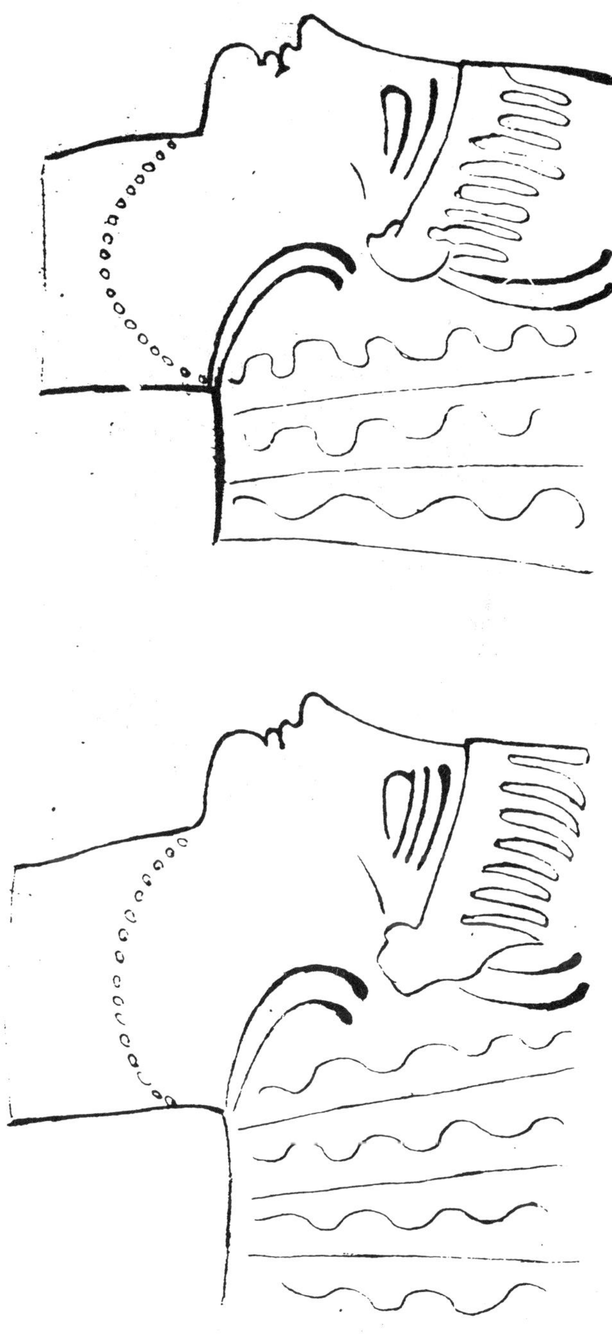

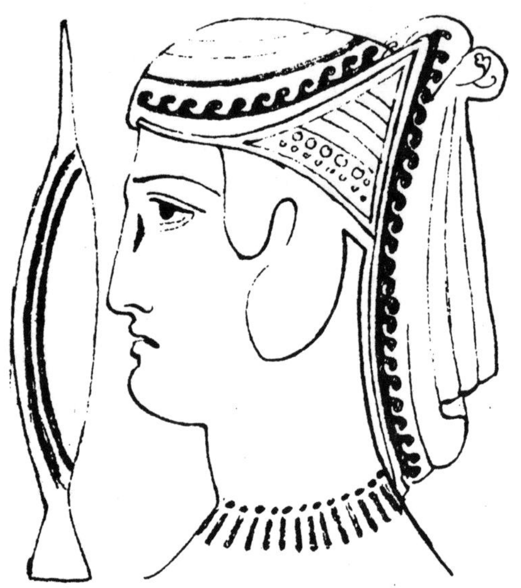

Index of Painters

Index of Museums